Power Player's Guide for Rodgers & Roland Organs

The complete step-by-step illustrated guide to mastering use of the tonal resources and internal/external memory

Nelson Dodge

Published by
Church Keyboard Center, LLC
Pasadena, CA
www.churchkeyboard.com

Library of Congress Cataloguing-in-Publication Data
Dodge, Nelson, 1957–
Power Player's Guide for Rodgers & Roland Organs
ISBN-13: 978-1490391205
ISBN-10: 1490391207

Photos of Rodgers and Roland products used with
permission of Rodgers Instruments, Inc.

Every attempt has been made to ensure that the
information and procedures in the Power Player's
Guide are technically accurate. Should you discover
any details that are inconsistent with your Rodgers/
Roland organ, please send a description of the issue to
the author at nelson@churchkeyboard.com. Corrections
and clarifications of procedures are available at
http://www.powerplayersguide.com

Contents

Index of Power Player Tips & Tricks

Acknowledgements

This book is the result of the efforts and contributions of many people. In addition to the Power Players noted above, to whom I most grateful for their generosity in sharing their ideas, I want to especially acknowledge Tony Ha for his careful and repeated proofreading, Dewey Kuhn, Rick Morales, Noel Jones and Lynne Ludeke for their input and encouragement, Dan Miller and John Posposil for their assistance with technical details, and the entire team at Rodgers Instruments for their dedication to and passion for creating the fine instruments that inspired this book.

Who is a Power Player?

Becoming a Power Player does not require extraordinary talent or performance ability. All you need is a desire to learn, experiment and explore the possibilities of the amazing Rodgers/Roland organs that are the subject of this book. With a little curiosity and imagination, *you* can be a Power Player!

Why would you want to be a Power Player?

Beyond the personal satisfaction you will feel, Power Players are redefining and expanding the role of the organist in modern worship and on the concert stage. With the versatility that comes from mastering the tonal capabilities of a Rodgers/Roland organ, Power Players are inspiring congregations in thriving churches, thrilling concert audiences, and reaching new levels of personal enjoyment at home—and keeping the organ relevant in the modern world of music.

Power Players aren't worried about the future of the organ—they derive confidence from their ability to use the power of the modern organ to greatest effect. This book reveals the simple secrets to becoming a Power Player. How far you take it is limited only by your creativity and imagination.

Free Power Player Coaching

Become a Power Player in 30 days or less with our free e-mail Power Player Coaching Program that guides you through this book. Sign up at **www.powerplayersguide.com**

Introduction

Your Rodgers/Roland organ contains the most powerful and versatile digital organ technology on the market today. The SSC (Sound System on a Chip) platform delivers an unprecedented amount of tonal resources and control *built in* to every Rodgers/Roland organ.

The revolutionary SSC technology combines the operating system, digital signal processing and sound samples on a single processor chip. All of the tonal resources in the organ are available to the organist all the time, instantly playable at the push of a button.

The *Power Player's Guide* explains in detail the concepts and techniques for using these powerful resources in your Rodgers/Roland organ to greatest effect.

Every Rodgers/Roland organ model contains extensive tonal resources beyond the nominal stop count. The stop count on any Rodgers/Roland organ is only a small portion of the complete tonal library available to the organist. The main stops (the blue bars in the chart below) represent less than 20% of the complete tonal library, with another 80%+ available in the Voice Palette and Library/User voices.

Although this plethora of tonal resources might seem "hidden," in reality these built-in voices have never been easier to access and use in the normal course of playing, thanks to the SSC architecture.

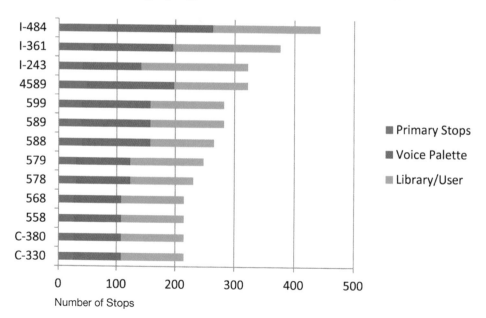

The *Power Player's Guide* applies to all Rodgers/Roland classical organ models built on the SSC platform (see below). Many of the concepts explained in the *Guide* apply to older Rodgers models (for example: *Voice Palette* and using a *MIDI* sound module), although the techniques may vary and not all features will be available. The following charts show the current system software versions as of the publication of this edition of the *Power Player's Guide*:

Infinity	Classic / Artist / 500
243LT / v. 2.06 (Mar 2013)	*Classic Series*
243MV / v. 2.06 (Mar 2013)	C-330 / v. 1.13 (Mar 2012)
243P / v. 2.06 (Mar 2013)	C-380 / v. 1.13 (Mar 2012)
361LT / v. 2.06 (Mar 2013)	558 / 568 / v. 1.05 (Oct 2012)
361MV / v. 2.06 (Mar 2013)	
361P / v. 2.06 (Mar 2013)	*Artist Series*
484LT / v. 2.03 (Apr 2013)	579 / *
484MV / v. 2.03 (Apr 2013)	589 / v. 2.40 (Oct 2013)
484P / v. 2.03 (Apr 2013)	599 / v. 2.40 (Oct 2013)
	4589 / *
	500 Series (Legacy)
LT = Lighted drawknobs	578 / v. 1.74 (Oct 2013)
MV = Moving drawknobs	588 / v. 1.74 (Oct 2013)
P = Platinum edition	
	version not known as of Dec 2013

Rodgers/Roland organs are designed for the demanding requirements of professional organists, whether used for service playing, concert performances or home practice. You will turbo-charge your playing by taking advantage of the vast tonal resources in your Rodgers/Roland organ using the techniques explained in this *Guide*.

This *Guide* shows you, in illustrated step-by-step detail, how to easily access and navigate the controls needed to unlock the full potential of your organ. Plus, you'll learn tips and tricks used by concert artists that fully exercising the capabilities of your Rodgers/Roland organ.

One final note: it is not the purpose of the *Power Player's Guide* to address specific registrational or tonal philosophies, but rather to fully equip *you* to explore and fulfill *your* tonal and registrational ideas and fully exercise the extensive capabilities of your Rodgers/Roland organ to take you anywhere you want to go in the world of organ sound color.

How to Use the Power Player's Guide

Your *Owner's Manual* contains the basic instructions for using the features and capabilities of your Rodgers/Roland organ. The *Power Player's Guide* goes beyond the *Owner's Manual* to explain in depth how and when to use the extensive tonal features and capabilities of your organ to their fullest effect.

There is minimal overlap between your *Owner's Manual* and the *Power Player's Guide*, so you should have a basic operational understanding of the controls on your organ model before reading this *Guide*.

Basic skills

The *Power Player's Guide* assumes that you are familiar with the basic controls on your organ, specifically:

- Stops and couplers
- General and divisional pistons, and toe studs where applicable

In addition to the basic controls and functions on your organ, you need to be able to comfortably navigate the system menus in the display window, using the MENU/SELECT and EXIT/VALUE knobs. You should be able to easily perform all of the following:

- Navigate to a specific menu
- Access the menu
- Select specific parameters
- Change the parameter values
- Exit the menus and return to the home screen

Although the appearance and location of the menu controls vary from model to model, they function exactly the same for all models. Below are photos of the Infinity (left) and Classic/Artist/500 Series (right) menu controls and a synopsis of how to use them:

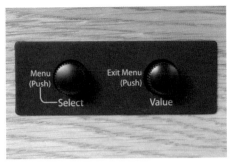

Infinity models

Classic/Artist/500 Series models

- **Menu** - *PUSH* to enter the menus and to select a specific menu item
- **Exit Menu** - *PUSH* to exit a menu, *PUSH* as many times as necessary to return to the home screen
- **Select** - to navigate the list of menus or parameters (after entering the menus or a specific menu item) *TURN* clockwise to move *down* the list, *TURN* counterclockwise to move *up*
- **Value** - *TURN* clockwise to move *forward* through the available options or to *increase* numerical values, *TURN* counterclockwise to move *backward* in available options or to *decrease* numerical values

Basic terminology

Stop vs. voice

On any Rodgers/Roland organ there is an important distinction between a stop and a voice. Unlike most organs where each stop always activates the same digital voice or rank of pipes, the stops on your Rodgers/Roland organ have the ability to play any of several voices (digital voice or rank of wind-blown pipes). Using and managing this multiplicity of voices is what makes your Rodgers/Roland organ so powerful. These two terms are used throughout this *Guide* as follows:

- *Stop* refers to the drawknob or tab *control* used to turn sounds (voices) on and off
- *Voice is* the specific sound that is heard when a drawknob or tab (stop) is on

Registration vs. combination vs. ensemble

These terms are closely intertwined. As used in this *Guide*:

- *Registration* refers to the group of stops that are on.
- *Combination* is a registration that has been saved on a piston and can be recalled during performance.
- *Ensemble* is the composite sound of the registration.

Online resources

Visit the *Power Player's Guide* web site at www.powerplayersguide.com for on-going updates and news, and to order additional copies of the

Guide. The web site is the source for the latest corrections, new features and addenda. You can also sign up for the free e-mail coaching program available to all readers.

www.PowerPlayersGuide.com

Rodgers Instruments web site is the source for the latest product information and to find a Rodgers dealer near you. Go to www.rodgersinstruments.com.

CHAPTER 1

The Rodgers Tonal Universe

1

Prerequisites

A basic familiarity with playing pipe and/or digital organs.

Chapter Outline

- The big idea
- Organizational architecture
- Visualizing the architecture

The big idea

Your Rodgers/Roland organ contains a whole universe of sound—all built into the console and available to use at the push of a button. Understanding how to use and navigate all of these tonal options is the focus of this *Power Player's Guide*.

Before exploring the specific techniques, it is helpful to understand how the voices are organized. All Rodgers/Roland SSC-based organs have a similar architecture. A clear understanding of the organizational architecture will help you master the techniques for any particular model.

The Primary Stops

In a pipe organ, pressing a stop tab or pulling a stop drawknob turns on a *rank* of pipes that produce a specific sound when a key is pressed. You play your Rodgers/Roland organ the same way: press the stop tabs or pull the drawknobs and the organ plays those sounds. In a Rodgers/Roland digital organ, the sounds you hear have been sampled from real wind-blown pipes and are being reproduced electronically.

If your Rodgers organ includes wind-blown pipes, some of the sounds you hear are made by the pipes.

But this is where the similarity with a pipe organ ends. Your Rodgers/Roland organ contains many more *voices*—sampled pipe organ and orchestral voices—that you can add to your ensemble or play as solo voices.

These additional voices are organized into various groups and are accessed in different ways.

Voice Palette

The first group of additional voices are found in the Voice Palette. These are alternate pipe organ voices available on every stop tab or drawknob. They may be used instead of the *default* primary voice that plays on that stop. Voice Palette voices provide tonal variety to your registrations.

Each stop has a specific set of Voice Palette voices that can be *mixed and matched* with other stops (and their Voice Palette voices) in any combination of your choosing. *Chapter 2* explains everything you need to know about using Voice Palette voices.

Library/User Voices

In addition to and separate from the Voice Palette, your Rodgers/Roland organ contains a substantial number of other pipe organ and orchestral voices that are available to be played in all divisions of the organ. These are the Library/User voices.

Library/User voices include *parameters* you control that change the tonal character of these voices, giving you virtually unlimited tonal possibilities. *Chapter 3* explains how to use Library/User voices to their fullest effect.

MIDI Voices

An external MIDI (*Musical Instrument Digital Interface*) sound module adds even more voice possibilities, in addition to the primary stops, and the Voice Palette and Library/User voices built in to your Rodgers/Roland organ.

A MIDI sound module typically includes a vast array of sounds, from organ, piano and orchestral voices, to synthesizers, sound effects and drum rhythm tracks. *Chapter 4* provides basic information about MIDI and explains the techniques for using a MIDI sound module with your Rodgers/Roland organ.

Visualizing the architecture

The various groups of built-in voices (Primary stops, Voice Palette and Library/User voices) are organized in a similar way in all Rodgers/Roland organ models. The controls for accessing these voices vary across the models as explained throughout the *Power Player's Guide*.

The following diagrams illustrate the organizational architecture for the Rodgers/Roland Classic models 558 / 568 / C-330 / C-380, which are tonally identical, and the Rodgers Infinity 361. These two diagrams are representative of the Artist/Classic and Infinity models' architecture, respectively.

Classic 558 / 568 / C-330 / C-380

- Total of 212 internal voices
- 27 stop tabs (27 primary voices / 81 Voice Palette voices) in three divisions (Great/Manual I, Swell/Manual II and Pedal)
- 6 USER/MIDI coupler tabs (2 per division) access 104 internal User voices OR external MIDI sound module voices (see *Appendix C*)

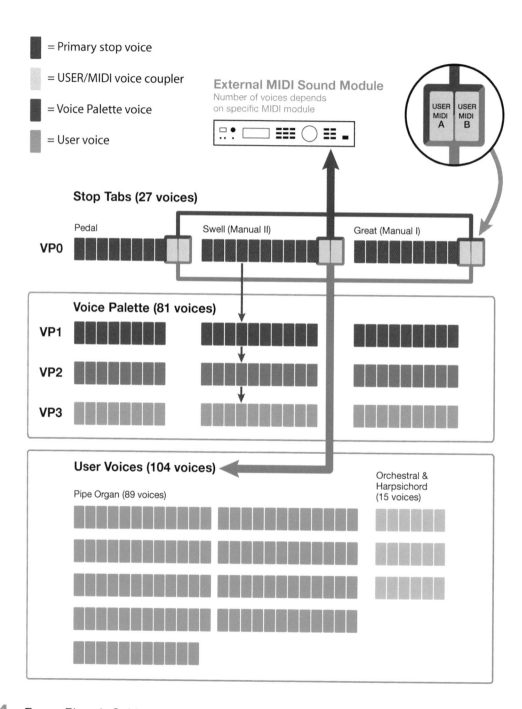

= Primary stop voice

= USER/MIDI voice coupler

= Voice Palette voice

= User voice

External MIDI Sound Module
Number of voices depends
on specific MIDI module

USER MIDI A   USER MIDI B

Stop Tabs (27 voices)

Pedal   Swell (Manual II)   Great (Manual I)

VP0

Voice Palette (81 voices)

VP1

VP2

VP3

User Voices (104 voices)

Pipe Organ (89 voices)

Orchestral & Harpsichord (15 voices)

Infinity 361

- Total of 376 internal voices
- 59 drawknobs & 2 pistons (61 primary voices / 135 Voice Palette voices) in five divisions (Great, Swell, Choir, Solo and Pedal)
- 9 Library access drawknobs (2 each Great, Swell, Choir and Pedal / 1 in the Solo) access 180 internal Library voices (see *Appendix C*)
- 8 MIDI coupler pistons access external MIDI sound module voices

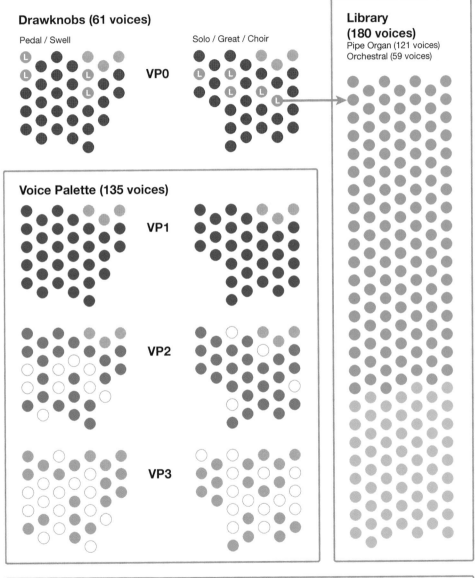

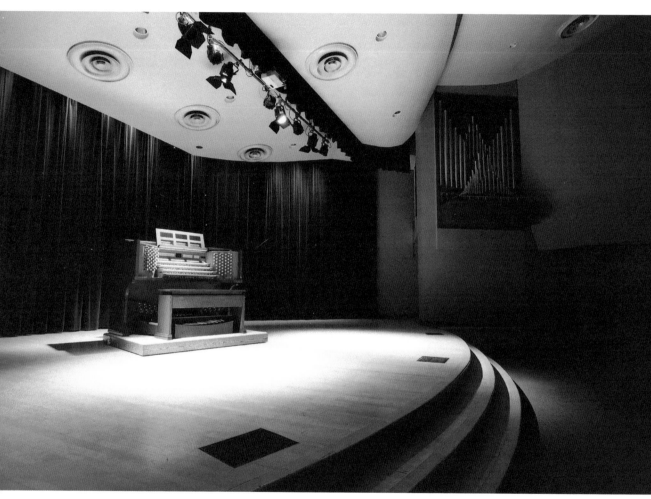

Azusa Pacific University School of Music (Azusa, CA) has the first Rodgers Infinity four-manual organ installed on a university campus in the United States. This installation features six ranks of windblown pipes for the Great principal chorus and selected Choir stops. Organ students develop their performance skills supported by the unlimited tonal possibilities of the Infinity organ. With their own USB memory stick, each student has instant access to all of their registrations when practicing or performing—a total of 1,188 combinations, with the ability to back up over 30,000 registration combinations on a single memory stick (See Chapter 7, External Combination Memory).

CHAPTER 2

The Voice Palette

Prerequisites

Familiarity with basic organ terminology (see pp. ix and x) and use of the controls on a Rodgers or Roland organ (refer to the *Owner's Manual* for your model and p. ix).

Chapter Outline

- Voice Palette concept
- Auditioning Voice Palette voices
- Achieving artistic results
- Default stops
- Changing the default stops
- Organ Type piston
- Voicing

Voice Palette concept

The Voice Palette was first introduced on Rodgers organs in 1995 with the model 960, a three-manual model of 72 stops and a total of 95 voices. Since then, the Voice Palette tonal options have continued to expand with each successive generation of Rodgers organs. Today, with the SSC-based models, the choices available to you are greater than ever.

The Voice Palette provides a selection of alternate voicing styles of the primary stop voice. For example, a stop marked Principal 8' will play a principal pipe tone at the 8' pitch with an American Classic voicing.

The Voice Palette voices also provide a principal pipe tone at 8′ pitch, but use a different sound sample with alternative voicing styles such as English, French Romantic or German Baroque. The Voice Palette is the most accessible and quickest way to create registrations of tremendous variety and subtlety with your Rodgers or Roland organ, especially when registering for repertoire of a specific style or period.

The power of the Voice Palette is in the ability to use *any* voice at *any* time—you are not limited to playing the primary and Voice Palette voices in a predetermined set of voices chosen by the manufacturer. You have the control to choose any Voice Palette voice that provides the result you want, both as a solo voice or as part of an ensemble.

Selecting Voice Palette voices works in tandem with using combination memory to instantly recall your registrations during performance (see **Chapter 6**) and the Default Stops and Organ Type features described in this chapter.

Registration: less is more

By Power Player Dr. Christoph Bull

I like to explore the individual stops of each organ, experimenting with single stops and combinations of two or three  stops. Ultimately, I pick stops based on how they sound, not necessarily what they're called. It is important to try alternatives and go through the full process of registering a piece. If a stop doesn't contribute to the ensemble, it probably muddies it, so I leave it off. Go for clarity.

Try sparser registrations even on big pieces. Sometimes a Principal 8′ or a Principal 8′ and Octave 4′ can provide enough substance for a forte passage. Sometimes a 2′ Principal is not necessary when a mixture is used. Be careful to not overuse mixtures and reeds. (Sometimes a 2 2/3′ stop can substitute for a mixture). Save the biggest registrations for the biggest moments.

The Rodgers Voice Palette and Library/User voices provide extensive options for achieving variety in a Principal 8′ and Octave 4′ ensemble. Try substituting any of the 8′ and 4′ principal voices in the Voice Palette in place of the default voice. Then experiment with the Library/User principal voices of similar pitch. Use the Level parameter to balance the two voices with each other. For more variation, see what effect the Warmth, Presence and Brilliance controls have on the ensemble.

And it doesn't stop there. All of the 16′, 8′, 4′ and 2′ Principal family Library/User voices can be made to speak at 8′ or 4′ by adjusting the Octave parameter, opening up even more options for experimentation.

When using voices from a MIDI sound module, try blending them with traditional organ stops. Use swell pedals and/or velocity parameters on the MIDI sounds to make them unobtrusive.

Be creative, fine-tune your ears and enjoy the process.

Web site: www.christophbull.com

Selecting a Voice Palette voice

On models with drawknob stop controls, pull the drawknob to turn on the stop.

On models with tab stop controls, press the bottom of the tab to turn on the stop.

The currently active Voice Palette voice is displayed. Turn the Value knob to select the desired Voice Palette voice.

The window displays the currently selected Voice Palette voice. This voice remains active until some other action changes the Voice Palette selection.

Note that the stop name engraved on the drawknob or tab is usually* the VP0 voice, with VP1, VP2 and VP3 being the alternate Voice Palette voices. Stops on Infinity models do not have a VP2 and/or VP3 for every stop—please refer to the tonal specification for your model.

VP0 is the factory default voice for each stop, however this can be permanently changed. (See *Changing the Default Stops* on p. 12).

*In some instances, an organ may be customized with engraved drawknobs or tabs that reflect a customized default stops specification. In these cases the engraved name on the drawknob or tab is the Voice Palette voice selected as the default voice for the stop in question.

Auditioning Voice Palette voices

Press keys on the keyboard while "dialing" through the Voice Palette voices. You will hear each Voice Palette voice instantly as it is selected.

Power Player Tip: to hear the effect of a particular stop's Voice Palette options on the entire ensemble sound, register all of the other stops for the ensemble and then activate the stop to be auditioned, which will display the Voice Palette for that stop. While playing, turn the VALUE knob to dial through the Voice Palette options and listen to the how the ensemble sound changes.

Related information

- *Chapter 4* - additional concepts for understanding and controlling which Voice Palette voice is active.

Achieving artistic results

Other brands of digital organs that offer multiple voicing options typically do not enable "mixing and matching" of the various alternative voices—the entire organ must be switched to the desired tonal "suite." This "suite" approach is an all or none tonal arrangement—you have no option but to use the stop voicings as determined by the organ manufacturer.

With your Rodgers/Roland organ you have the ultimate choice of which voicing alternative to use for every stop in any registration. Along with this unfettered control comes the responsibility to ensure that the registrations you create are artistically pleasing.

Registrations should not be rote or purely theoretical, i.e., choosing all the "French" voicings because the repertoire is French. Rather, registrations are about the resulting sound and effect that is created—let your ears by the ultimate judge of what actually sounds "French"...and good. Always use the audition technique described above to refine your registrations for the best effect.

The Voice Palette (combined with the Library/User voices explained in *Chapter 3*) is the ultimate in artistic control. Using it effectively is at the core of being a Power Player.

Default Stops

The *default* stop is the Voice Palette voice that is selected for each stop when:

- The organ is initially powered on
- The Default Stops piston is pressed (Infinity / 588 / 589 / 599 / 4589)
- The Cancel piston (0) is pressed and held for several seconds (this action also turns off any stops that are on)

Activating any stop following any of the above actions causes the stop to play the default voice. Any subsequent actions that effect Voice Palette selections (General or Divisional pistons, Organ Type piston) may change the Voice Palette selection for any stop.

VP0 is the factory default for every stop. VP0 is the Voice Palette voice that is engraved on the stop drawknob or tab. Any stop can be *customized* to default to VP1, VP2 or VP3 (see *Changing the default stops* below).

The Default Stops piston does not turn off any stops and couplers that are on—stops and couplers that are on, remain on, but the voice of some or all stops may change.

An alternate method of resetting to the default stops is to press and hold General Cancel for several seconds. With this method all stops are turned off *and* reset to the default voice. This method also turns all couplers off.

Using the General Cancel method to reset to the default stops differs from briefly pressing General Cancel, which turns all stops and couplers off, but does *not* change the Voice Palette selection. Following a General Cancel, each stop will continue to play the *last* selected Voice Palette or Library voice when turned on manually.

Changing the default stops (voices)

The factory default stops setting is VP0 for every stop, in other words, the name engraved on the stop tab or drawknob. The default stop can be changed to any of the Voice Palette options. Customizing the default stops causes the organ to reset to your *customized* default stops when any of the following occurs:

- The organ is initially powered on
- Pressing and holding General Cancel (0) for several seconds
- Pressing the Default Stops piston (Infinity / 588 / 589 / 599 / 4589)

Your Rodgers/Roland representative can customize the default stops for Artist and Classic Series models. The default stops are user-programmable on Infinity models.

Getting the perfect ensemble

By Power Player Dr. Frances Nobert

Certain passages in the organ literature often call for a very specific tonal chorus: it might be principals, strings, flutes or reeds. Whatever the need, assembling the tonal resources with the precise effect desired—and sometimes with a tonal quality characteristic of a  particular period of organ building—is not possible using the basic organ specification available. Even with the ability of the Voice Palette to provide alternate voicing styles, you may still find that you lack the quantity of voices, and at multiple pitches, to create the desired chorus.

The Library/User voices on your Rodgers organ provide the ultimate solution. With two voices in each division, these can be combined with another stop in the division to create just about any 16', 8' and 4' chorus you could ever imagine.

For example, *Cortège et Litanie* by Marcel Dupré calls for a 16', 8' and 4' String chorus on the first page. I achieve a very specific sound that I like on my Rodgers Model 588 with the following registration:

III / Swell
  Viola Celeste 8'

II / Great
  Chimes

I / Choir
  Unda Maris II 8'
  User A - 067 16+8+4 Celli VI
  III > I [Swell to Choir]

Pedal
  Montre 32'
  Subbass 16'
  Bourdon 8'
  I > Pedal [Choir to Pedal]
  III > Pedal [Swell to Pedal]

For the User A voice on the Choir, set the volume parameter to 65.

The effect of this String chorus conveys the subtlety that accurately represents the intent I believe Dupré envisioned for this passage.

Web site: www.francesnobert.com

Setting the default stops

Select the Voice Palette voice for each stop that you want to be the default (see p. 9).

While holding the SET piston, press GENERAL CANCEL (0)—the **Save Setup** screen appears (below).

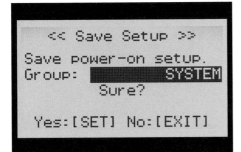

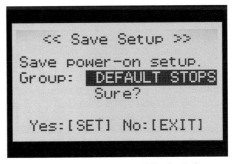

Turn the VALUE knob until Default Stops is displayed in the highlighted field.

Press the SET piston to save your customized default stops.

The screen displays the message "Executing..."

13

Organic Type piston (Infinity & 588 / 589 / 599 / 4589)

The Organ Type piston selects a pre-determined Voice Palette voice for each stop that changes the organ specification to one of four tonal styles:

- American Eclectic
- English Cathedral
- French Romantic
- German Baroque

Selecting an organ type will override the currently active Voice Palette selections for all stops. Both stops that are on and off are affected by the Organ Type piston. After selecting an organ type, the current Voice Palette selection for any individual stop will display in the window when the drawknob is pulled or stop tab pressed down.

The Voice Palette selection for any particular stop will be changed by any subsequent action that changes the state of each stop

- Manually selecting a different Voice Palette voice (individual stop)
- Recalling a registration with a general or divisional piston
- Pressing the Default Stops piston
- Pressing and holding the General Cancel (0) piston for several seconds (resets to default Voice Palette selections)

It's important to remember that the particular Voice Palette selection for any given stop is dynamic—affected by any of the above actions, including using the Organ Type piston to change all of the Voice Palette selections simultaneously. In other words, selecting any of four Organ Types does *not* permanently set the Voice Palette option for each stop to the pre-determined selection for the particular Organ Type.

The Organ Type feature is best used when setting new combinations to perform specific repertoire. First, select the desired Organ Type, then manually register combinations and save them to general pistons. Keep in mind that recalling a previously saved piston will change the Voice Palette selections, most likely *not* the Voice Palette selections for the Organ Type you chose.

Refer to *Appendix B* for a listing of the Organ Type Voice Palette selections for the Infinity 361 and Models 588 / 589 / 599. The built-in Organ Types are not editable. See the Power Player Tip on page 15 for creating your own custom Organ Type.

Selecting Organ Type

Press the Organ Type piston—the piston will light and the Organ Types appear in the window (below).

Turn the SELECT knob to select one of the four Organ Types. The Organ Type highlighted instantly becomes the active organ type.

Play the organ with any registration to hear the tonal changes as you change the Organ Type.

Press the Organ Type piston again to return to the previous screen display.

The currently active Voice Palette voices for the selected Organ Type remain active until changed by another action, such as recalling a saved registration with a piston or pressing the Default Stops piston (p. 11).

Create a custom Organ Type

By Power Player Dr. Jung-A Lee

Set the Voice Palette option for each stop that you want to use as your custom organ type specification.

Now set this to a general combination memory piston. Use a memory level that is not regularly used for performance, but convenient to get to, such as level 20 on 500 Series and 99 on Infinity. Keep notes on which pistons recall your custom organ types.

Note that it does not matter if the stops are on or off when you set the general piston—the Voice Palette options you selected will be saved.

Hint: to differentiate this special general piston from others, you might save it with all the stops on as a visual cue that it is a custom organ type piston. When you recall the piston, press General Cancel to turn the stops off—your custom organ type remains active.

Web site: www.musicmissioninternational.org

Voicing

Voicing is the process of adjusting various tonal characteristics of the sound of a voice in order to:

- Adjust the volume level so that the voice blends appropriately with other voices—the *ensemble*
- Compensate for frequency response dynamics of the room
- Change the tonality/timbre of the voice for stylistic preferences

Voicing can involve much more, but in general it is the finishing and polishing of the organ sound—both individual stops and the ensemble—that makes your organ sound its best in the acoustic space where it is installed. This is an expert and detailed process that your organ provider must do for the primary stop voices and the Voice Palette voices. Rodgers/Roland organs can be voiced on several levels:

- Division level—sound level and equalization can be set for all voices in each division
- Stop (rank) level—changes the sound for all the notes for a particular voice
- Note level—changes the sound for an individual note of a particular voice.

Your organ provides stop (rank) level voicing controls for each of the Library/User voices. You will learn how to use these controls in the next chapter.

Related information

- *Chapter 3* - Library/User voices provide for rank level voicing control by the organist
- *Chapter 4* - MIDI voices provide for rank level voicing control by the organist

Library / User Voices

Prerequisites

Familiarity with basic organ terminology (see pp. ix and x) and use of the controls on a Rodgers or Roland organ (refer to the *Owner's Manual* for your model and p. ix).

3

Chapter Outline

- Library / User voice concept
- How to access the voices
- The power of parameters

Library / User voice concept

The Library/User voices are additional pipe organ and orchestral sounds available to use as solo voices or as part of ensemble registrations. These voices also provide a number of powerful parameters that enable altering them in useful ways. Used to their fullest artistic effect, these parameters enable virtually unlimited sound variations.

How to access the voices

The number of Library/User voices and the way they are accessed differs according to organ model (see *Appendix C* for a complete listing of the Library/User voices for all models).

Each Rodgers Infinity model has 180 Library voices. These voices are accessed via two drawknobs in each division (one drawknob in the Solo) marked with an "L."

Each one of the Library drawknobs can access the entire set of Library voices. The voices are numbered for convenient reference.

Library voices 001 - 121 are pipe organ voices, organized from low to high pitch in five general tonal groups:

- Principals, stings, flutes & mutations
- Mixtures
- Reeds
- Ensemble voices (multiple rank/ multi-pitch ensembles)
- Theatre organ voices

Library voices 200 - 258 are orchestral voices, organized as follows:

- Keyboards
- Orchestral strings
- Orchestral brass
- Orchestral winds
- Choral
- Bells & chimes
- Percussion / drums

See *Appendix C* for a complete listing of Library voices.

Selecting a Library voice

Pull the drawknob to which you wish to assign a Library voice.

Turn the VALUE knob clockwise to dial through the Library voices. Note that the first few voices are the Voice Palette voices for the selected drawknob. The Library voices are identified with a three digit number as shown.

The selected Library voice may now be saved on a general or divisional piston as a solo voice or as part of an ensemble registration.

Rodgers 558 / 568 / 578 / 588 and Roland C-330 / C-380 models have 104 User voices. Rodgers 579 / 589 / 599 / 4589 models have 124 User voices. These voices are accessed via the two USER/MIDI stop tabs in each division. Models 588 / 589 / 599 / 4589 access the User/MIDI voices via two pistons in each division.

Each one of the USER/MIDI tabs or pistons can access the entire set of User voices. The voices are numbered for convenient reference on Artist Series models.

User voices 001 - 090 are pipe organ voices, organized from low to high pitch in five general tonal groups:

- Principals, stings, flutes & mutations
- Mixtures
- Reeds
- Ensemble voices (multiple rank/ multi-pitch ensembles)
- Theatre organ voices

The remainder of the User voices are keyboard and orchestral voices. See *Appendix C* for a complete listing of User voices.

Selecting a User voice

Press the USER / MIDI tab to which you wish to assign a User voice. Models 588 / 589 / 599 / 4589, press the User/MIDI piston.

Because the USER / MIDI tabs are used to access both User voices and external sound module voices, the source must be set to *USER* when setting a User voice.

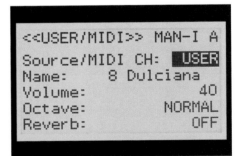

Turn the SELECT knob to highlight Source/MIDI CH. Then turn the VALUE knob to select USER.

```
<<USER/MIDI>> MAN-I A
Source/MIDI CH:    USER
Name:      8 Dulciana
Volume:           40
Octave:       NORMAL
Reverb:          OFF
```

Turn the SELECT knob to highlight the voice Name, then turn the VALUE knob to select a User voice.

The power of parameters

Each Library/User voice includes a number of voicing parameters that are user-adjustable. It is important to set at least some of the values when using a Library/User voice. The voice will initially play with either the default values or the values last used, either of which may or may not be appropriate for the repertoire of the moment. This is especially true for the Volume parameter: the default is 40, which is often too soft for most ensemble uses for many of the Library/User voices.

Setting the values for various parameters is easy and opens up infinite tonal possibilities for your registrations. When you save a Library/User voice on a general or divisional piston, all of the parameter values are saved and the values you set will be instantly recalled when the piston is activated.

When using Library/User voices, observe the following:

- The same Library/User voice may be used on multiple stops simultaneously with different values for any of the parameters
- The Library/User voice must be saved to a piston in order to recall the values you set
- After initially saving a combination that includes a Library/User voice, if you make further changes to any parameter(s), remember to save the combination again to capture the updated parameter values, otherwise the values last saved will be recalled when the piston is activated (i.e., after saving the combination, if you make adjustments to the parameter values and then decide that you *don't* like the change, *don't set the piston again*—simply press the piston to recall the combination with the original parameters you saved)

Parameter descriptions

Division (Infinity only)

Assigns the voice to play in the A or B speaker system for the division. Do not use this parameter if your organ does not have both an A and B speaker system.

Name

The name of the voice. Pipe organ voices include the pitch level: 8', 4', etc.

Volume   Value Range: Off, 1 to 127

The volume level for the voice. The default level is 40. Adjust the volume level in the context of the ensemble that the voice is part of. This parameter works in conjunction with the Velocity parameter to ultimately determine the volume level of any particular note as it is played.

Octave   Value Range: -2 to +2

The octave the voice will sound at. Default value is Normal. At the normal level an 8' pipe organ voice will speak at piano pitch. At +1 the voice will speak at a 4' pitch. At -1 the voice will speak at 16' pitch, and so on. All together, the Octave parameter enables a five octave range for each voice.

Coarse Tune   Value Range: -12 to +12

Adjusts the pitch in semitone steps.

Fine Tune   Value Range: -50 to +50

Adjusts the pitch within a range of +/- 50 cents. 100 cents is the equivalent of a semi-tone. This parameter enables tuning the note up to a quarter-tone sharp or flat.

Warmth   Value Range: -10 to +10

Adjusts the low-frequency tone of the sound. This parameter, used in conjunction with the Presence and Brilliance parameters, enables considerable voicing of the tonality/timbre of the voice.

Presence   Value Range: -10 to +10

Adjusts the mid-frequency tone of the sound. This parameter, used in conjunction with the Warmth and Brilliance parameters, enables considerable voicing of the tonality/timbre of the voice.

Brilliance   Value Range: -10 to +10

Adjusts the high-frequency tone of the sound. This parameter, used in conjunction with the Warmth and Presence parameters, enables considerable voicing of the tonality/timbre of the voice.

Reverb   Value Range: OFF, 0 to 127

Adjusts the reverb depth of the sound. The default for this parameter is OFF.

Velocity   Value Range: KBD, EXP, 2 to 127

This setting determines the Velocity value used when playing the voice. This parameter works in conjunction with the Volume parameter to ultimately determine the volume level of any particular note as it is played. A lower Velocity value produces lower volume, higher Velocity produces higher volume.

- KBD - the velocity with which the key is struck will determine the volume of the sound. KBD produces the best results when used with piano, orchestral and percussion voices. Do not use KBD for organ voices.

- EXP - the volume level is determined by the position of the expression pedal. Use this value for organ voices for which you want to control volume level with the expression pedal.

- 2 to 127 - select a fixed Velocity value when you want the voice to speak at a consistent volume, regardless of the key velocity. A fixed Velocity level is not recommended for piano, orchestral or percussion voices.

Create a custom celeste stop

By Power Player Hector Olivera

In my opinion, an organ can never have too many celeste stops. The Library/ User voice capabilities on Rodgers/Roland organs enables you to create unique celeste stops.

Each division (except the Solo division) provides two Library/ User voices that can be played together. By using the tuning capability of these voices you can create your own celeste. Here's how to do it.

Select the same voice from the Library/User voices on each of the two Library/User stops in the division where you want the celeste to play. Access the tuning parameter for one of the voices and set the value to 7. Likewise, access the tuning parameter for the other voice and set the value to -7.

What you have just done is tune the first voice sharp and second one flat, creating a two-rank celeste stop when these two voices are played together. The amount of detuning should be roughly equal for each voice, in other words, if one is -5 the other should be +5. Play the two voices together when setting the tuning parameter so you hear the effect as you increase or decrease the amount of detuning.

When you are satisfied with the result, save the registration to a general piston for instant recall during performance.

Web site: www.hectorolivera.com

Setting parameters

Activate the Library drawknob or User tab or piston and turn the VALUE knob to select the desired voice (as described earlier in this chapter).

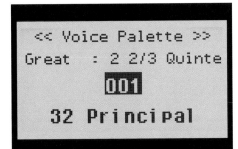

The currently selected Library/User voice is displayed. Note: on Artist/Classic models, the parameters screen is displayed when the stop is turned on—skip to the next column.

Infinity only: press the SET piston—the parameters screen will appear in the window (below).

Turn the SELECT knob to move from one parameter to another.

Turn the VALUE knob to change the value for any parameter.

Play notes while making changes to the parameter values to hear the effect on the sound.

Save the Library/User voice to a piston (as a solo voice or as part of an ensemble registration) to recall later with the parameters you set.

3

23

The Bob Tall 85-key piano

By Power Player Dr. Robert Tall

The Infinity and Artist organs have a beautiful grand piano voice in the Library...but only a 61-note keyboard, which deprives you of the bottom and top octave you would have on an 88-key piano.

Use my trick to create an 85-key piano for "full scale" pianistic playing. This works best on a three-manual organ, but can be adapted to a two-manual when necessary.

Setting up your 85-key piano uses one Library stop each in the Swell, Great and Choir.

First, set a Library/User stop in the Great to play the #200 Grand Piano. Set the volume at the level you need and make a note of it.

Now set a Library/User stop in the Swell to play the #200 Grand Piano. Set the volume the same as the Great and the Octave parameter to +1.

Lastly, do the same with a Library/User stop in the Choir, but set the Octave parameter to -1.

Save this setting to a General piston. When this General piston is recalled you will instantly have an 85-key piano.

So how does it work? Simple. You've got the grand piano playing on all three manuals: on the Great at the standard piano pitch. On the Choir an octave lower and on the Swell an octave higher.

To demonstrate your 85-key piano, play an arpeggio from the very bottom of the keyboard to the top. Start at low C on the Choir, continue the arpeggio on the Great and end on the top octave of the Swell.

To complete your 85-key piano, use the kick switch on the Great/Choir expression shoe as the sustain pedal. The kick switch has various functions. In the Expression Pedal menu set it to SUSTAIN.

Alternatively, you can use a toe stud as a sustain pedal. The function of each of the toe studs is programmable by your Rodgers/Roland organ representative. Select the toe stud you wish to have function as the sustain and ask your Rodgers representative to assign the SUSTAIN function to that toe stud. If the function of that toe stud is one you want to keep, it can be moved to another toe stud.

Web site: www.roberttall.com

CHAPTER 4

External MIDI Module Voices

Prerequisites

Familiarity with basic terminology (see pp. ix and x) and use of the controls on a Rodgers or Roland organ (refer to the *Owner's Manual* for your model and p. ix).

Chapter Outline

- MIDI overview
- MIDI implementation on Rodgers/Roland organs
- Using a MIDI sound module
- Taking your MIDI skills to the next level

4

MIDI overview

MIDI is an acronym for *Musical Instrument Digital Interface*. MIDI is a *protocol* that defines a standard set of codes that all MIDI capable instruments send and receive. In other words, MIDI is a language that digital instruments use to communicate with each other.

Rodgers organs have been MIDI capable from the very beginnings of MIDI as a result of the leadership of the Roland Corporation in creating the MIDI standard in the 1980s. 2013 marked the 30th anniversary of MIDI, which is now ubiquitous throughout the music industry—at last count over 700 companies make MIDI-compatible products.

MIDI has the ability to control a variety of devices, from keyboards to lighting to sound. This chapter explains how to use MIDI to play additional voices and sounds from the keyboard of your Rodgers/Roland organ using an external MIDI-capable sound module.

When to use MIDI

With the primary stop voices, Voice Palette and Library/User voices already built in to your Rodgers/Roland organ, you already have a substantial amount of tonal resources suitable for the requirements of the vast majority of worship music and organ repertoire.

When these built-in tonal resources are not enough to support your performance needs, the seamlessly integrated MIDI capabilities of your Rodgers/Roland organ provide the ability to easily access an entire universe of instrumental and synthesized sounds—literally thousands of sounds.

There is no limit to how additional voices can be used to subtly or dramatically augment your tonal palette. Just a few basic examples:

- Subtle orchestral strings add lushness to a registration of organ celeste stops
- Use orchestral percussion for a flashy ending
- Create an entire rhythm section for a complete "pop" experience
- Use an ethnic/world instrument for a completely different or unique sound
- Go retro with classic synthesizer sounds
- Rock out with an electric guitar solo
- Keep it classic with an acoustic guitar
- Use a classic tone wheel organ for a jazz or gospel sound
- Take your listeners "out of this world" with unusual electronic sound effects

The possibilities are endless and only limited by your imagination.

How MIDI works

As a communication protocol, MIDI enables your Rodgers/Roland organ to control a sound module to play the desired voices. At the simplest level the organ sends data to the module, which in turn sends audio (voice and notes) back to the organ.

- Recalling a registration with a piston that includes a voice in the MIDI sound module sends a voice code, or *program change* code, to the module that identifies the voice to be played.

- Pressing a key generates MIDI key code, or *keying data*, that is sent to the module causing the module to generate the note being played using the selected voice.

- The module sends an audio signal to the organ that becomes part of the audio being generated by the organ.

Connecting a MIDI sound module

The wiring connections between the organ console and the MIDI module follow the above communication requirements:

- A MIDI data cable connects the MIDI OUT on the organ console to the MIDI IN on the sound module, enabling the organ to send MIDI data to the module.

- Two quarter inch audio cables (stereo left and right) connect the AUDIO OUT on the module to the Auxiliary AUDIO IN on the organ console.

4

When is a voice MIDI or not MIDI?

The term MIDI is sometimes used to generally refer to non-organ voices (piano, orchestral, percussion, etc.), i.e, MIDI voices. Strictly speaking, MIDI is the communication protocol that enables accessing *any* kind of voice in a sound module using a controller keyboard (the organ).

The term MIDI becoming synonymous with non-organ voices likely derives from the early implementation of MIDI on Rodgers organs when external sound modules only had orchestral type voices, and the organs only had organ voices.

Today, MIDI is used to access both organ and non-organ voices available in external sound modules. Further, organ and non-organ voices are built in to all Rodgers/Roland organs and accessed directly without the use of MIDI.

The extensive list of User and Library voices built in to Rodgers/Roland organs should not be confused with voices accessed via MIDI, although they behave in similar ways. Library/User voices are internal to the organ and do not need MIDI codes (PC, MSB & LSB) to use these voices.

You will note on the Artist/Classic organs that the USER/MIDI stop tabs/pistons function as an *either/or* stop, depending on how you set the Source parameter in the menu. The USER/MIDI stop can play an internal USER voice *or* an external voice from a MIDI sound module.

MIDI implementation on Rodgers/Roland organs

MIDI provides sixteen channels for musical instruments (and other devices) to communicate with each other. Your Rodgers/Roland organ assigns two MIDI channels per division to access an external MIDI sound module. In other words, you can play one or two voices from a sound module per division at the same time. Channels are assigned as follows:

- Great MIDI A - channels 1 through 16 (assignable)
- Great MIDI B - channel 5
- Swell MIDI A - channel 2
- Swell MIDI B - channel 6
- Choir MIDI A - channel 4
- Choir MIDI B - channel 8
- Pedal MIDI A - channel 3
- Pedal MIDI B - channel 7

The MIDI standard specifies a basic set of voices that use the same program change codes in most instruments. These voices are referred to as General MIDI 2, or GM2. Beyond this basic set of GM2 voices, a sound module or keyboard contains many more voices, or *patches*, that are specific to that module or keyboard. Refer to the *Owner's Manual* for your MIDI sound module for the list of program change codes needed to access the voices from your organ (see the next section *Using a MIDI sound module*).

Similar to Library/User voices, MIDI voice selections are captured and recalled via registrations saved on pistons. Unlike, Library/User voices, MIDI voices do not couple between divisions.

Using a MIDI sound module

To play a voice from an external MIDI sound module, the desired voice is assigned to the MIDI A or MIDI B coupler in the division where you want to play the voice. Each voice has a unique *address* that consists of three codes that range from 0 to 128:

- Program Change (PC) - the specific *voice*
- Most Significant Bit (MSB) - the *bank*, or group, of voices
- Least Significant Bit (LSB) - the voice *variation* within the bank

Despite the technical names of the MIDI voice codes, just think of them as the nine-digit address of each voice in the sound module, very similar to a postal code (which consists of a five-digit Zip code plus a four-digit extension in the U.S.) or a telephone number (which consists of a three-digit area code plus the local seven-digit telephone number in the U.S.).

In addition to the nine-digit voice address, you can set a number of parameters that affect how the voice will sound. These parameters are similar to the Library/User voice parameters (see **The power of parameters** in **Chapter 3**). As with the Library/User voices, it is important to adjust the Volume parameter so that the voice balances with the ensemble you are using. The parameter values are recalled along with the voice on the general or divisional piston where it is saved.

Using a MIDI sound module in performance

The seamless MIDI integration in your Rodgers/Roland organ enables saving all required MIDI parameters on general and divisional pistons. This makes it possible to instantly recall these MIDI settings during performance as part of a registration ensemble.

Each MIDI coupler can be set up with a different voice and parameter values on a series of pistons, instantly changing the voice and its parameters with each piston change. With two MIDI couplers per division and the ability to change voices with each piston change, performances of great variety and complexity can be as simple as using the NEXT piston!

Assigning a voice to a MIDI coupler piston

Press the MIDI coupler piston you want to set. The piston will illuminate and the MIDI parameters appear in the window (below).

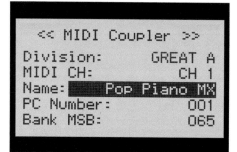

With the Name *or* the PC Number highlighted, turn the VALUE knob to select a different voice. If the voice you want is in a different bank (MSB), see the next step for changing MSB and LSB parameters.

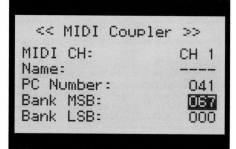

Turn the SELECT knob to select the PC, MSB and LSB parameters, then turn the VALUE knob to enter the address values for each of the parameters. Note that the voice name may or may not display. When the PC Number, MSB and LSB values are entered, the voice will play when the MIDI piston is lit. To be able to recall this voice later, complete the next step, otherwise the MIDI coupler settings can be superseded by other actions.

To save the MIDI piston settings so that the voice you have selected can be recalled later, save it on a general or divisional piston (see *Chapter 6*).

Assigning a voice to a MIDI coupler tab

Press the MIDI coupler tab you want to set. The USER/MIDI window appears (below).

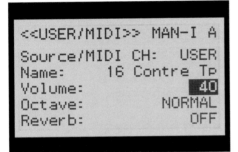

If (as shown) the tab is currently set for an internal USER voice, you must switch the Source to MIDI to use this tab as a MIDI coupler as shown in the next step.

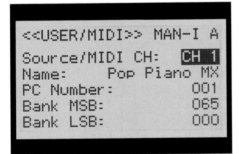

Turn the SELECT knob to highlight the Source (USER) parameter, then turn the VALUE knob to select CH x. The USER/MIDI tab is now in the MIDI coupler mode.

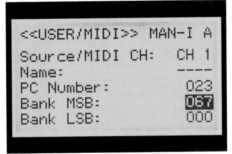

Turn the SELECT knob to highlight the Name parameter, then turn the VALUE knob to select a different voice—note that the PC Number changes as the Name changes. If the voice you want is in a different bank (MSB), see the next step for changing MSB and LSB parameters.

Turn the SELECT knob to select the PC, MSB and/or LSB parameters, then turn the VALUE knob to enter the address values for each of the parameters. Note that the voice name may or may not display. When the PC Number, MSB and LSB values are entered, the voice will play when the MIDI tab is lit.

To save the MIDI tab settings so that the voice you have selected can be recalled later, save it on a general or divisional piston.

4

Selecting voices using the Quick Key method

The keys of the Great, Swell, and a portion of the Pedals (or Choir on a three manual model) are designed to select a PC code when the MIDI coupler is flashing. The following instructions explain how to use the *quick key* method to set a MIDI coupler.

Press the MIDI coupler that you want to set so that it is illuminated *and* the parameters are displayed in the window. Press and **hold** the SET piston. The MIDI piston or tab will flash.

While the piston or tab is flashing, press the key that corresponds to the Program Change code for the voice you want (refer to the MIDI chart for your sound module). The PC number will change in the window. Release the SET piston.... the MIDI coupler stops flashing.

The keys correspond to MIDI PC codes as follows:

- Great - PC 1-61
- Swell - PC 62-122
- Pedal (or Choir) - PC 123-128

Note that the MSB and LSB are not set with this method. If the voice you want is in a different bank (MSB or LSB) than what is presently set, manually change the MSB and or LSB values.

Auditioning voices

You can audition voices while the parameters are still visible in the window.

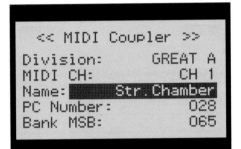

To audition by voice name: use the
SELECT knob to highlight the Voice
parameter, then use the VALUE knob to
dial through different voices.

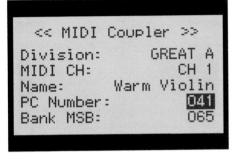

To audition by MIDI address: use the
SELECT knob to highlight the PC
(and/or MSB/LSB) parameter, then use
the VALUE knob to select PC Numbers.

As each voice is selected, play notes on
the keyboard to hear the voice.

Setting and saving parameters

Press the MIDI coupler (piston or tab) for which you want to change parameters. (If the piston or tab is already illuminated, turn it off and then back on). The MIDI parameters appear in the window (below).

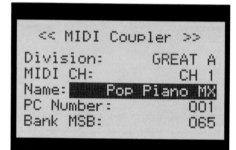

Use the SELECT knob to select the parameter(s) to be changed (below).

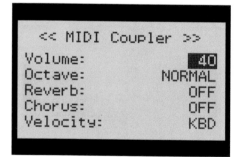

The default Volume level is 40. It should be adjusted so that the volume of the selected voice is balanced with the particular ensemble with which it is being used.

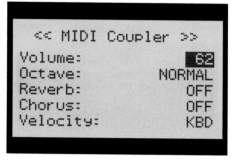

Turn the VALUE knob to change the value of the parameter.

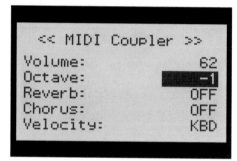

The Octave parameter provides for moving the pitch of the voice up or down by as much as two octaves, which is useful for achieving a variety of artistic effects. Turn the SELECT knob to select the Octave parameter, then turn the VALUE knob to change the value.

Changes made to MIDI parameters are temporary until saved on a combination piston for instant recall later.

Taking your MIDI skills to the next level

Your Rodgers/Roland organ can do much more with MIDI than simply accessing voices on an external sound module. With more advanced skills you can:

- Record the MIDI data of a live performance for automatic playback
- Edit a MIDI data file on a PC or Mac to correct/change the performance

These advanced skills are beyond the scope of this *Guide*. Many books are available that explore the full capabilities of using MIDI for performance, editing and orchestration.

Use divisional pistons for favorite sound module voices

By Power Player Bob Salisbury

When you use sound module voices often in service playing, you'll most likely develop a short list of voices that you use frequently as solo voices that would be convenient to have instantly available at any moment. This is an instance where the divisional pistons come in handy.

Use memory level 1 (or another memory level that you always use for your service playing) and set each divisional piston in the division you want to use for the solo voices. For instance, you might set the pistons as follows: 1-piano, 2-oboe, 3-flute, 4-harp, 5-guitar. Pressing piston 1 sets up the keyboard to instantly be a piano when you need it. Piston 2 or 3 instantly gives you a solo oboe or flute that you can accompany on another manual with an appropriate registration, even switching back and forth between the oboe and flute by pressing piston 2 or 3.

If you have a three-manual model you could set the divisional pistons on both the Swell and Great to a selection of favorite solo voices giving you the option of having a different solo voice playing on the Swell and Great at the same time, while accompanying on the Choir.

E-mail: salisburysounds1@verizon.net

Making the most of registration possibilities

By Power Player Dr. Fred Swann

The art of registration is a complex and fascinating subject. The ability to search out and present the "best" sounds to an audience is one of the most critical standards by which organists, and the organs they play, are judged.

It is possible to obtain completely satisfying sounds by using only those  heard when you draw stops identified by the name on the knobs—without ever using voices from the Voice Palette or Library/User voices. Listen carefully to the sound of each stop individually, and then in combination with those of their specific tonal family.

In choosing registration, the most important resource often neglected by too many organists is physical—his/her ears. Many factors influence the sound of an organ—digital or pipe. Drawing the stops suggested on printed music does not guarantee a good effect. Before playing listen critically and analyze the sound.

Depending on the composition being performed it is often possible, with minimal changes, to make the sound more beautiful and, in many cases, more appropriate. Attempt to keep to the basic tonal intention of the composer, or let your imagination and ear tell you what sounds best.

With your Rodgers/Roland organ this can be achieved by being adventurous and exploring the various methods of altering and/or increasing the variety of sound. Use the Voice Palette variations available on each stop to produce subtle and effective results. One of endless examples possible: in some full registrations changing the

Pedal 32' Contre Bombarde (on models that have this stop) to the 32' Ophicleide (VP1) can produce both a more full and clean effect (you can also use a Library/User voice to achieve this effect).

To enhance individual and ensemble sounds, take the time to carefully search through the extensive Library/User voices available. Any of these can easily be set on the User A/B tabs or pistons on Classic and Artist Series and 578/588 models, or the drawknobs in each division that are indicated by a "L" on the Infinity models.

Many treasures are available. On my Infinity 484 I have assigned an entire memory level to special solo stops and ensembles from the Library voices. By easy reference I can quickly identify a variety of solo reed or flute voices, principal or string ensembles and special use combinations without having to search through the entire Library list.

In building ensembles "less is more, or fewer is better" is always a reliable rule. *Full organ* does not mean "pulling out all the stops." Doing so often produces an ugly or distorted effect.

Principal and reed choruses are intended to be used together in ensembles, and flutes and strings work well together. Combining stops from all four families except for a special reason or effect is not recommended. (And never, ever, add celeste stops to Principal or Chorus Reed stops or ensembles.)

Finally, be aware that the combinations you have set in one room may not be suitable in another. Always remember to take your ears along when you go to play an organ that by model number appears to be identical to another. Many factors can require even subtle changes for your registration to be effective.

http://www.powerplayerguide.com

CHAPTER 5

Navigating All the Tonal Resources

Prerequisites

Ability to select Voice Palette voices (see *Chapter 2*), Library/User voices (see *Chapter 3*), and MIDI voices (see *Chapter 4*).

Chapter Outline

- Concept of state
- Current state of a stop
- Actions that change state

Concept of state

The concept of the *state* of each stop on your Rodgers/Roland organ is fundamental to mastering control of the extensive tonal resources available. It is *the most* important thing you can learn from this *Guide*.

On a pipe organ, each stop is either off or on. Thus, the state of the stop is either *off* or *on*. Your Rodgers/Roland organ is similar: each stop can be in an *off* or *on* state. However, since each stop is capable of playing multiple voices, the state of the stop includes a second attribute: the *voice* that is currently active. The active voice is determined by a variety of actions, which we'll explore momentarily.

The chart below shows the eight possible states of a stop on an

Artist/Classic organ. The number of states for any particular stop on an Infinity organ varies depending on the number of Voice Palette voices.

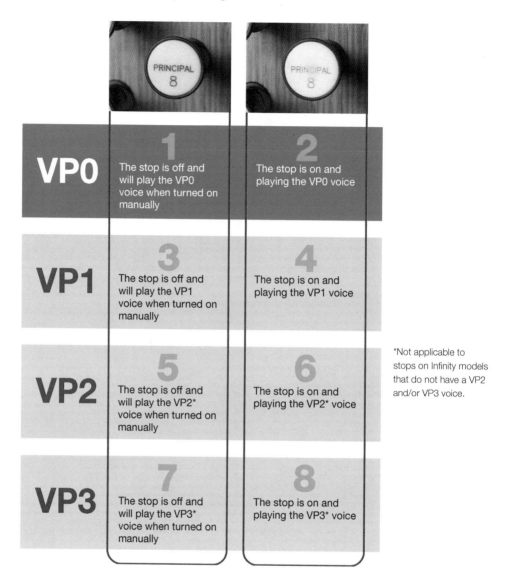

VP0	**1** The stop is off and will play the VP0 voice when turned on manually	**2** The stop is on and playing the VP0 voice
VP1	**3** The stop is off and will play the VP1 voice when turned on manually	**4** The stop is on and playing the VP1 voice
VP2	**5** The stop is off and will play the VP2* voice when turned on manually	**6** The stop is on and playing the VP2* voice
VP3	**7** The stop is off and will play the VP3* voice when turned on manually	**8** The stop is on and playing the VP3* voice

*Not applicable to stops on Infinity models that do not have a VP2 and/or VP3 voice.

Current state of a stop

When you save a registration on a general or divisional piston, *both* the on/off state *and* the voice state of *each* stop is saved. In other words, one of the eight states described above is captured for *every* stop. The Voice Palette selection of stops that are in the off state is saved, along with the stops that are in the on state. After recalling the combination on a piston, any stop subsequently turned on manually will play the Voice Palette voice that was selected when the combination was saved.

This affords you the opportunity to *prepare* stops in a combination to be manually pulled. However, it also requires that you be fastidiously aware of the current voice state of *all* stops when setting combinations.

Actions that change state

Actions that occur as you play your Rodgers/Roland organ are constantly changing the state of some or all the stops. The on/off state is obvious— it's the voice state that isn't immediately apparent, until you play it or display the Voice Palette in the window. With a modest amount of planning, practice and awareness, you'll know the current voice state of the stops at any moment.

Last action prevails

With the state of the stops constantly changing and evolving, the key to knowing the current state of any given stop is to be aware of the sequence of actions performed, with particular attention to the most recent action that changed the state of *some* or *all* of the stops.

For the sake of clarity, this *Guide* uses the following terms to differentiate the types of actions that change the state of stops:

- **Global** - an action that changes the state of *all* stops
- **Divisional** - an action that affects the state of all stops in a *single* division
- **Stop** - an action that changes the state of a *single* stop

Actions that change global state

- Pressing a General piston to recall a registration—changes on/off *and* voice state for all stops (see p. 44)
- Pressing the Default Stops piston—changes voice state (only) for all stops (see p. 11)
- Pressing the General Cancel piston—sets on/off state to *off* for all stops, does *not* change voice state

- Holding the General Cancel piston for a few seconds—sets on/off state to *off* for all stops, *and* changes voice state (to the default VP) for all stops (see p. 11)
- Changing the organ type with the Organ Type piston—changes voice state (only) for all stops (see p. 14)

Actions that change divisional state

- Pressing a Divisional piston to recall a registration—changes on/off *and* voice state for all stops in the division (see p. 44)

Actions that change stop state

- Manually changing the Voice Palette selection for any stop—affects only the stop displayed in the window (see *Chapter 2*)
- Manually selecting a Library/User voice for any of the Library/User stops—affects only the stop displayed in the window (see *Chapter 3*)

An example

The following illustrates a hypothetical sequence of actions that change state at the global, divisional and stop levels.

- *Global*—General Piston 1
  Recalls on/off *and* voice (VP0, VP1, VP2, VP3 or Library/User voice) state of all stops
  (as previously set on General 1)

- *Global*—General Piston 2
  Recalls on/off *and* voice state (VP0, VP1, VP2, VP3 or Library/User voice) of all stops
  (as previously set on General 2)

☐ *Divisional*—Swell Divisional Piston 1

Recalls on/off *and* voice (VP0, VP1, VP2, VP3 or Library/User voice) state of all Swell division stops (as previously set on Swell Divisional 1)

- *Global*—General Piston 3

Recalls on/off *and* voice (VP0, VP1, VP2, VP3 or Library/User voice) state of all stops (as previously set on General 3)

 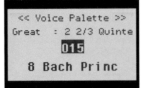

▪ *Stop*—Manually turn on a Library stop and select the 8′ Bach Principal: Infinity = voice 015, Artist/Classic = voice 010

On/off state is on, voice state changes to Library voice #15 - 8′ Bach Principal

▪ *Stop*—Turn off the Library stop (from the previous action)

On/off state is off, voice state *remains* on Library voice 8′ Bach Principal

- *Global*—General Cancel

  Changes on/off state to off for all stops, does *not* change voice state

- *Global*—Press and hold General Cancel for five seconds

  Changes on/off to off for all stops, resets voice state of all stops to default voice

How to get more 16' and 32' pedal stops

By Power Player Dan Miller

Need a 16' or 32' pedal stop with more bass than what you get from the pedal division stops? This tip is particularly useful on the Classic models that don't have a 32' pedal stop. Select a voice from the Library/User voices and "voice" it to be the stop you need.

For example, turn on one of the pedal division User A/B tabs or on the Infinity models, one of the Library stops. Turn the VALUE knob to select 006 Lieblich Gedeckt.

On Infinity models, while "006 LibGed" is displayed on the screen, press the SET piston. You will now see a menu of parameters that you can adjust. On Classic and Artist Series models the parameters are automatically displayed in the window when a User voice is selected.

Turn the SELECT knob to select the "Warmth" parameter. Turn the VALUE knob to set the Warmth parameter to 10.

You will also want to adjust the volume level to achieve an appropriate balance of the Library/User voice with the other stops you are using.

This setting can be saved to a divisional or general piston (as part of an ensemble registration) for instant recall with the values you have set.

Web site: www.danmillermusic.com

CHAPTER 6

Combination Memory

Prerequisites

An understanding of the tonal resources available on your organ (see *Chapters 2, 3* and *4*) and the concept of state (see *Chapter 5*).

Chapter Outline

- Basic concept
- Saving registrations
- Using memory levels
- Recalling combinations during performance
- Next & Previous pistons
- Organizing combination memory
- Documenting your registrations
- Changing toe stud functions

6

Basic concept

Combination memory gives you the ability to save *combinations* of stops for instant recall during performance. The saved combinations are recalled via the general and divisional pistons and toe studs. Your Rodgers organ provides multiple *levels* of internal memory for saving combinations, enabling you to save many times the number of combinations as there are pistons.

Saving registrations

Manually registering combinations of stops takes time, especially when you refine your registrations using Voice Palette and Library/User voices. Capturing your registration on a general or divisional piston (also known as *setting* a piston) enables instantly recalling the registration during performance when it would be impractical or impossible to make such changes manually.

Using a series of general pistons enables recalling your registrations in sequence with the Next and Previous pistons, instantly changing the sound of the organ at predetermined points during performance (see p. 48).

Setting a piston

When you set a piston, the organ is actually saving much more information than simply the stops and couplers that are on. When you set a piston, the following are saved for instant recall later:

- On/off state of each stop
- On/off state of each coupler
- On/off state of each MIDI coupler
- Voice state of every stop, i.e., Voice Palette and Library/User voice (see *Chapters 2* and *3*)
- Parameter values of all selected Library/User voices (see *Chapter 3*)
- Parameter values for the dedicated MIDI couplers (see *Chapter 4*)
- Parameter values for the USER/MIDI couplers that are in MIDI mode (see *Chapter 4*)

Note that the voice state is saved for *all* stops (whether they are on *or* off), including values for the Library/User and MIDI parameters. This enables preparing stops to be turned on manually.

For example, you might want to manually add a big reed voice to an ensemble after recalling the registration with the piston. You can select the Voice Palette voice that you want for the big reed and, although the stop is off when you set the piston, the specific Voice Palette voice you selected is saved and ready to be turned on manually.

If the big reed voice is selected from the Library/User voices, or a

MIDI sound module, you should also ensure that all of the parameters are set appropriately for the combination. After recalling the registration (without the big reed playing), when you manually activate the stop (or MIDI coupler) to turn on the big reed, all the parameters will be exactly as you set them.

How to set a piston

Rodgers/Roland capture action works like most other organs' capture action. To save a registration that is currently active on the stop draw-knobs or tabs:

Press and **hold** SET, then press and release the General or Divisional piston. Release the SET piston.

6

Using memory levels

The internal memory in your Rodgers/Roland organ enables you to save many more combinations than there are pistons. Combination memory is organized into *levels*, referred to as Memory Level 1, Memory Level 2, and so on. The current memory level is displayed in the window.

This home screen shows that the combination memory is currently using memory level 12.

Amount of memory

Organ Model	Memory Levels	Total General Combinations
C-330 / C-380	20	100
Artist / 5x8	20	200
Infinity	99	1,188

Navigating memory levels

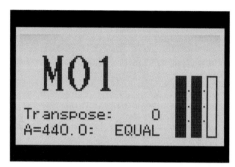

The organ initially powers on with Memory Level 1 active

M+ piston moves up one memory level each time it is pressed

M- piston moves down one memory level each time it is pressed

Scrolling through memory levels

Holding the M+ or M- piston for a few seconds will move through the memory levels continuously (incrementing or decrementing).

When moving upward through the memory levels, when you get to the highest memory level for your Rodgers/Roland model, pressing the M+ piston will move to Level 1.

Likewise, when moving downward through the memory levels, when you get to Level 1, pressing the M- piston will move to the highest memory level for your Rodgers/Roland model.

Recalling combinations during performance

Use the M-/M+ pistons to select the memory level where you saved the combinations you want to use.

Press the first piston to recall the combination you saved. Continue pressing pistons as needed during your performance to recall combinations previously saved.

Next & Previous pistons

The Next and Previous pistons (and toe studs) are the power tools of many concert organists. Properly prepared, these pistons simplify the performance of a work that involves many (dozens or even hundreds) of registration changes.

The concept is simple: save your combinations in the sequence they will be used, starting with General 1 and moving to General 2, then General 3 and so on. The sequence can continue uninterrupted up to the maximum number of combinations possible for the amount of combination memory for your organ (see table on page 46).

The Next piston is used to step through the combinations in sequence. The Previous piston is available to move backward in the sequence should the need arise by accident or design.

The genius of the Next piston is fully realized during performance: all registration changes are made by pressing the *same* piston—no need to think about which piston you pressed last or need to press next: simply press the Next piston to move to the next registration.

Infinity and Artist models also provide a Next and Previous toe stud, which performs the same function as the pistons and enables using your foot to trigger the registration change when your hands are too busy to press the piston.

Setting combinations for use with the Next/Previous pistons

Use the M- / M+ pistons to select the memory level to start saving the registration sequence.

Save the first combination on General 1, then save the next combination on General 2, then General 3 and so on. Continue saving combinations in sequence without skipping any pistons.

When you have saved a registration to the highest numbered General piston, press the M+ piston to advance to the next memory level. Then continue saving registrations, starting with General 1, then General 2 and so on. Continue using additional memory levels as needed, making sure to move directly to the next memory level. It is essential to *not* skip any piston or memory level when setting up a sequence that will be triggered using the Next piston.

6

Organizing combination memory

With so much combination memory built in to your Rodgers/Roland organ, it is helpful to have an organizational plan for the memory levels. When multiple organists use the organ, assigning a group of memory levels to each organist is a logical plan.

If you are the only organist, then you have the luxury of using all the memory levels however you wish. Your plan might look like this:

- M01 - Generic service playing: soft registrations and a standard hymn build sequence
- M02 - Choir anthem
- M03 - Funeral service settings

- M04 - Wedding service settings
- M05 to 09 - Reserved for substitute/visiting organists
- M10+ - Levels used for specific repertoire

When multiple organists use the organ, a plan similar to the above could be used, with memory levels 10 and above assigned to specific organists in blocks, where M10 to M14 is organist A, M15 to M19 organist B, and so on depending on the number of memory levels available on your organ.

When your need for memory levels exceeds the number available, use an external memory stick to expand the combination memory available. See *Chapter 7* for all the Power Player techniques for using memory sticks to create unlimited combination memory.

Documenting your registrations

A word to the wise: keep good notes. At the least, a title or brief description of the memory level will help you stay organized. Your notes can go further and describe each piston and registration details, including any MIDI settings and parameters.

Suffice to say you should document to the level of detail that you find useful and will need to use the combinations again.

Changing toe stud functions

Infinity, Artist and 578/588 models feature programmable toe studs, that is, the ability to assign the function you desire to each toe stud. You can choose the function you want for each toe stud and arrange them in a layout that works best for you.

Contact your Rodgers representative for assistance with reassigning toe stud functions. Your representative can also help you change the labels on the toe studs as necessary.

The available toe stud functions are summarized below by model.

Artist / 500 Series	578 / 579	588 / 589 / 599	4589
Number of toe studs	*10*	*10*	*10*
Generals	1-10	1-10	1-10
Pedal divisionals	1-5	1-5	1-5
Swell to Pedal (reversible)	✓	✓	✓
Great to Pedal (reversible)	✓	✓	✓
Choir to Pedal (reversible)	N/A	✓	✓
Swell to Great (reversible)	✓	✓	✓
Choir to Great (reversible)	N/A	✓	✓
Swell to Choir (reversible)	N/A	✓	✓
Solo to Swell (reversible)	N/A	N/A	✓
Solo to Great (reversible)	N/A	N/A	✓
Solo to Choir (reversible)	N/A	N/A	✓
Next	✓	✓	✓
Previous	✓	✓	✓
Sustain	✓	✓	✓
Full Organ (reversible)	✓	✓	✓
32' Montre (reversible)	N/A	✓	✓

Infinity	243	361	484
Number of toe studs	*10*	*24*	*23*
Generals	1-10	1-12	1-12
Pedal divisionals	1-5	1-5	1-5
Swell to Pedal (reversible)	✓	✓	✓
Great to Pedal (reversible)	✓	✓	✓
Choir to Pedal (reversible)	N/A	✓	✓
Swell to Great (reversible)	✓	✓	✓
Choir to Great (reversible)	N/A	✓	✓
Swell to Choir (reversible)	N/A	✓	✓
Solo to Great (reversible)	N/A	N/A	✓
Next	✓	✓	✓
Previous	✓	✓	✓
Sustain	✓	✓	✓
Full Organ (reversible)	✓	✓	✓
32' Bombarde (reversible)	N/A	✓	✓
32' Bourdon (reversible)	✓	✓	✓

6

The Rodgers four-manual model 4589 crowns the Artist Series and offers a total of 322 voices composed of 51 primary stops, 147 Voice Palette voices and 124 User voices.

CHAPTER 7

External Combination Memory

Prerequisites

A working knowledge of combination memory (see *Chapter 6*) and ability to navigate the menus (see pp. vii and ix).

Chapter outline

- Basic concept
- Combination memory
- Managing combination memory files

Basic concept

Your Rodgers/Roland organ has two kinds of memory: *internal* and *external*. *Chapter 6* described the techniques for using the *internal* combination memory built into your organ. In this chapter you'll learn how, when and why to use *external* USB memory (also known as a *thumb drive*, *flash drive*, or *memory stick*) to extend the capacity of internal memory and add important and useful capabilities when using combination memory.

For sake of simplicity, we'll refer to external memory simply as *USB memory*. When referencing the physical USB memory media we use the term *memory stick*.

USB stands for *Universal Serial Bus*, a technical term that describes the communication protocol (standard) used to read and write data to USB memory. USB memory is solid state (no moving parts), high capacity (up to many gigabytes), very compact, inexpensive and highly reliable. Almost too good to be true...but it is!

Most computers can read and write to USB memory, which enables copying data files saved from your organ to your computer for added safety and management of your combination files.

Combination memory

With the hours invested in creating combinations and saving them in internal memory, you will save yourself much grief by making backups. An additional benefit is that your saved combinations can be used on a compatible Rodgers/Roland organ via the memory stick.

Because the specifications of each Rodgers Infinity, Artist and Classic model are standardized, combinations saved on one organ will work on any other Rodgers/Roland organ of the same model. This is especially useful for concert artists who perform a variety of repertoire.

For instance, you can work out your combinations on one Infinity 361, save the combinations to a memory stick and use those same combinations directly from the memory stick on any other Infinity 361.

The Classic models interact with USB media slightly differently (see below) but the general principle of interchangeability of saved combinations applies.

Managing combination memory files

(Infinity, Artist and 578 / 588)

Infinity, Artist and 578 / 588 models save combination memory to USB memory by individual memory level. Using the memory management tools available in the menus, you have extensive flexibility to organize, save and interchange combinations you have worked out for various repertoire and service playing.

Up to 26 sets of all internal memory levels can be saved to a single memory stick. Each set is saved to a folder on the memory stick labeled A, B, C .... Z. Each folder contains only the memory levels that have been saved to it. As you plan your combination memory backups, keep in mind that you can use as many of the 26 available folders as you like, with each folder containing as few or as many of the internal memory levels as needed.

Infinity / Artist / 578 / 588

External combination memory

- 26 folders per memory stick, labeled A through Z
- Each folder holds up to 99 memory levels for Infinity models, 20 memory levels for models Artist and 578 / 588
- File size: 20KB +/-

File structure

📁 RODGERS

   📁 A [...Z]

      📄 MBANK001.DAT

      📄 MBANK002.DAT

      📄 MBANK ...

      📄 MBANK099.DAT *[file numbering stops at 020 for Artist / 578 / 588 models]*

7

When using USB memory to save combinations, your intention to use USB memory strictly as a backup or for live performance determines how and when to save your combinations, as explained below.

Using USB memory for archival/recovery backup

Make a *backup copy* of your combinations on USB memory for archival and recovery purposes when you plan to use the organ's internal combination memory for performance. In this case, work out your combinations and save them to internal memory just as you normally do.

When the combinations are finalized, or at any point that you wish to make a backup copy, insert a memory stick and save the memory levels you want to back up using the SET method (see p. 59). When you have saved all the memory levels needed, immediately remove the memory stick, label it and put it in a safe place. These combinations can be restored to the organ's internal memory later whenever needed.

A backup copy of a memory level can only be saved to a particular folder on a memory stick once—using the SET method to save a *subsequent* version of the memory level will *not* update the file on the memory stick. To make subsequent (update) or multiple backup of a particular memory level, use any of the following methods:

- Save to a different folder on the memory stick that does already contain the memory level in question
- Use a different memory stick
- Delete the memory level on the memory stick and then save it again using the SET method. To delete the memory level, use the Delete procedure on p. 61 or use a PC to view the memory stick directory and delete the memory level file. As an added safeguard, use your PC to also copy the file to the PC before deleting it on the memory stick.

When using USB memory to make backup copies of your memory levels, one must be mindful of what folders and memory levels are already on the memory stick. *A previously saved memory level on a memory stick cannot be overwritten in the same folder using the SET procedure.* Good record keeping is essential to avoid unpleasant surprises!

Using USB memory for performance

When you plan to use combinations stored on a memory stick for live performance, work out your combinations with the memory stick inserted in the organ while setting your combinations. All of the memory levels you are using, along with the changes/edits you make to individual pistons as you work out your combinations, are saved to the memory stick *only*—not the internal memory in the organ. When you are finished setting your combinations, remove the memory stick.

To access the combinations you just saved, you must have the memory stick inserted in the console on which you are performing. As you recall combinations, any memory levels saved on the memory stick override internal memory. If you select a memory level *not* saved on the memory stick, internal combination memory is used.

Keep in mind that a memory stick holds up to 26 folders. Upon inserting the memory stick, the organ reads from and writes to the folder last used. See the instructions on p. 58 for selecting folders.

Copying a memory level from or to USB memory

Once a memory level is saved to USB memory you have the option of loading it back into internal memory in the organ, or updating the USB memory with the current combinations saved on that memory level in internal memory.

When loading from USB memory to internal memory you must select both the internal memory level to write to and the saved memory level on the memory stick that will be copied. In addition to simply restoring a set of combinations to the *same* internal memory level, this gives you the ability to *move* combinations from one level to another in internal memory. See the instructions on p. 60 for copying memory levels.

Deleting a memory level on USB memory

When a copy of a memory level on USB memory is no longer needed, it may be deleted. See the instructions on p. 61 for deleting memory levels.

7

Selecting the USB memory folder

When working with USB memory, either for performance or saving/copying/deleting memory levels, you must first select the active folder to use on the memory stick.

Insert a memory stick.

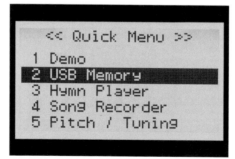

Push the MENU knob and turn to navigate to and highlight Menu 2 - *USB Memory*. Press the SELECT knob to access the menu.

Note: Rodgers recommends formatting USB memory before using with your organ. Although many memory sticks will read and write without formatting, it's good practice to always format a new memory stick before using it. To format, go to Menu 14 and select the Format USB Memory option.

Upon entering the menu, you see summary information for folder A (below). Here you can see that five memory levels have been saved to folder A.

Note that this screen does not show which memory levels have been saved. It is advisable to keep written records, however, you can see which memory levels have been saved in each folder by viewing the file structure of the memory stick on a PC or by using the Copy Memory Bank function in Menu 14 to see (albeit one at a time) the memory levels that are saved in the folder you select below.

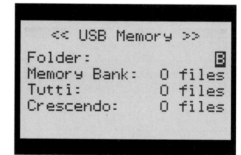

Turn the VALUE knob to select any folder from A to Z. This folder will remain the active until changed or the memory stick is removed.

Saving combination memory to USB memory (SET method)

Insert the memory stick before performing this procedure. The procedure is the same for both an archival/recovery back up and creating combinations on a memory stick to use in live performance.

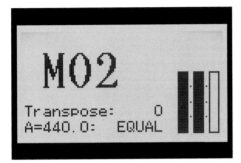

Select the Memory Level to be backed up using the M-/M+ pistons.

Press General piston 1 to recall the combination.

Press and **hold** SET, then Press General piston 1.

If the memory stick has an LED indicator, it will flash, indicating that the memory level has been saved.

Caution: after saving a memory level to the USB memory and while the memory stick remains plugged in, any further changes made to combinations are saved ONLY to the USB memory, internal combination memory is NOT updated.

- If your intent is to have a back up copy of the internal combination memory only, *remove the memory stick immediately* when finished saving memory levels.

- If your intent is to use the USB memory for live performance and updating the internal memory is not necessary, *leave the memory stick plugged in and continue editing your combinations.*

7

Copy Memory Level

Insert a memory stick and select a folder (A-Z) before performing this procedure (p. 58).

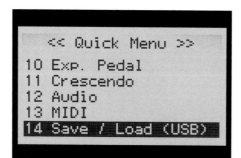

Push the MENU knob and turn to navigate to and highlight Menu 14 - *Save/ Load USB*. Push the SELECT knob to access the menu.

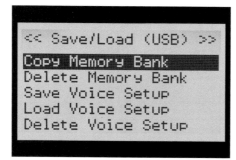

Turn the SELECT knob to highlight *Copy Memory Bank*, then push to enter.

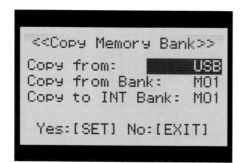

Turn the SELECT knob to highlight *Copy From*. Turn the VALUE knob to select:

- **USB** if you want to copy from the memory stick to internal memory

- **INTERNAL** if you want to copy an internal memory level to another internal memory level. Note: it is not necessary to have the memory stick inserted when copying internal memory levels.

Turn the SELECT knob to highlight *Copy from Bank*, then turn the VALUE knob to select the memory level you wish to copy.

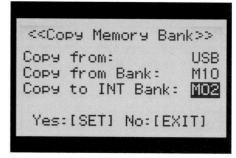

Turn the SELECT knob to highlight *Copy to INT Bank*, then turn the VALUE knob to select the internal memory level to which you wish to copy.

Press SET to copy.

Deleting memory levels

Insert a memory stick and select a folder (A-Z) before performing this procedure (p. 58).

Push the MENU knob and turn to navigate to and highlight Menu 14 - *Save/ Load USB*. Push the SELECT knob to access the menu.

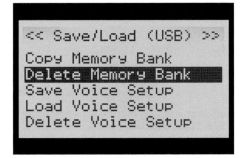

Turn the SELECT knob to highlight *Delete Memory Bank*, then push to enter.

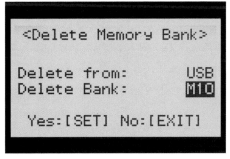

Turn the VALUE knob to select the memory level to be deleted.

Press SET to delete.

7

Managing combination memory files
(Classic)

The Rodgers/Roland Classic models save the entire set of 20 combination memory levels to USB memory as a single file. A single memory stick can save up to 999 combination memory files, each containing the entire contents of the 20 memory levels.

Using the management tools available in the menus, you have the ability to back up and restore combination memory, and also copy a specific memory level from USB memory to a selected level in internal memory.

Classic

External combination memory
- 999 files per memory stick, labeled 001 through 999
- Each file contains all 20 memory levels
- File size: 100KB +/-

File structure

📁 RODGERS [or C330, C380]
- 📄 MBANK001.DAT [or RC3A_001.DAT]
- 📄 MBANK002.DAT [or RC3A_002.DAT]
- 📄 MBANK ...
- 📄 MBANK999.DAT [or RC3A_999.DAT]

These models only read internal combination memory during performance. Combinations you have saved on a memory stick must be loaded into internal memory when you wish to use them.

When doing a performance that requires more than 20 memory levels, you can manage combination memory requirements by dividing your repertoire into groups that use 20 or fewer memory levels. Work out the registrations for each group and save that set of combinations as a separate file on the memory stick. As you complete each group of repertoire in the performance, load the combinations for the next group from the memory stick. Loading a combination file can be done in a few seconds.

Note that the Load Memory Bank function loads all 20 memory levels (see p. 65). The Copy Memory Bank function enables copying a single memory level from a memory stick or an internal memory level to an internal memory level (see p. 66-67).

Although the Roland C-330 might seem physically petite, it is a robust organ providing a total of 215 voices and 20 combination memory levels, the same as the other Classic Series organ models.

Saving internal combination memory to USB memory

Insert a memory stick before performing this procedure.

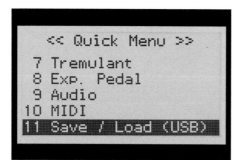

Push the MENU knob and turn to navigate to and highlight Menu 11 - *Save/Load USB*. Push the SELECT knob to access the menu.

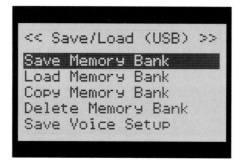

Turn the SELECT knob to highlight *Save Memory Bank*, and push to enter.

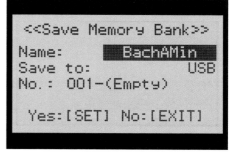

You can assign a custom name to the file that will be stored in USB memory. See Appendix A for instructions on naming files. Note: the name that appears is the one that was used in the last save operation.

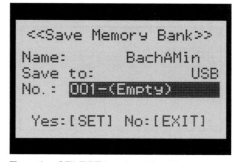

Turn the SELECT knob to the No. parameter, then use the VALUE knob to select the number of the back up file (999 files are available). Caution: select a number that is indicated as "Empty" (as shown above) unless you intend to overwrite a previously saved set of combinations.

Press the SET piston to save the combination data.

> *Note: Rodgers recommends formatting USB memory before using with your organ. Although many memory sticks will read and write without formatting, it's good practice to always format a new memory stick before using it. To format, go to Menu 11 and select the Format USB Memory option.*

Loading combinations from USB memory to internal memory

Insert a memory stick before performing this procedure.

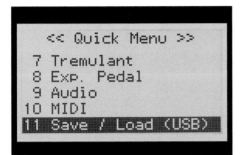

Push the MENU knob and turn to navigate to and highlight Menu 11 - *Save/ Load USB*. Push the SELECT knob to access the menu.

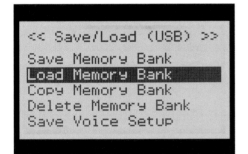

Turn the SELECT knob to highlight *Load Memory Bank*, and push to enter.

Turn the SELECT knob to highlight the No. field. Turnt the VALUE knob to select the file you wish to load. ***Caution: all internal memory levels will be over-written!***

Press the SET piston. A confirmation message will appear. Press the SET piston again to start the load.

7

Copying a memory level from USB memory to internal memory

Insert a memory stick before performing this procedure. Push the MENU knob and turn to navigate to and highlight Menu 11 - *Save/Load USB*. Push the SELECT knob to access the menu.

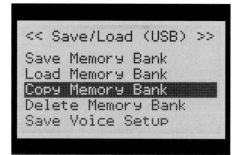

Turn the SELECT knob to highlight *Copy Memory Bank*, and push to enter.

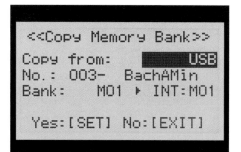

Turn the SELECT knob to highlight *Copy From*, then turn the VALUE knob to select *USB*.

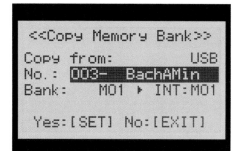

Turn the SELECT knob to highlight *No.*, then turn the VALUE knob to select the back up file you wish to copy from.

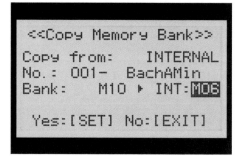

Turn the SELECT knob to highlight *Bank*, then turn the VALUE knob to select the the USB memory level you want to copy.

Turn the SELECT knob to highlight *INT*, then turn the VALUE knob to select the internal memory level to which you want to copy the combinations from USB memory.

Press the SET piston. A confirmation message will appear. Press the SET piston again to start the copy.

Copying a memory level from one internal memory level to another

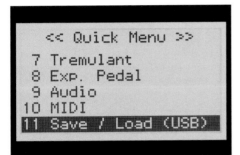

Push the MENU knob and turn to navigate to and highlight Menu 11 - *Save/ Load USB*. Push the SELECT knob to access the menu.

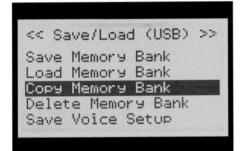

Turn the SELECT knob to highlight *Copy Memory Bank*, and push to enter.

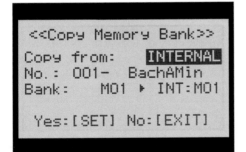

Turn the SELECT knob to highlight *Copy From*, then turn the VALUE knob to select *INTERNAL*.

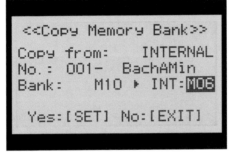

Turn the SELECT knob to highlight *Bank*, then turn the VALUE knob to select the internal memory level you want to copy.

Turn the SELECT knob to highlight *INT*, then turn the VALUE knob to select the memory level to which you want to copy the combinations.

Press the SET piston. A confirmation message will appear. Press the SET piston again to start the load.

7

Deleting memory files on USB memory

Insert a memory stick before performing this procedure.

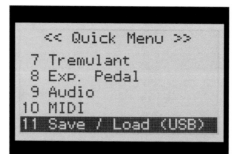

Push the MENU knob and turn to navigate to and highlight Menu 11 - *Save/Load USB*. Push the SELECT knob to access the menu.

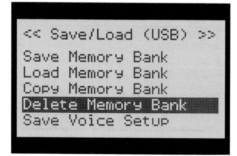

Turn the SELECT knob to highlight *Delete Memory Bank*, and push to enter.

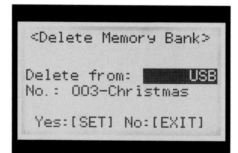

The Delete from value should be set to USB.

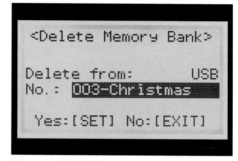

Turn the SELECT knob to highlight *No.*, then turn the VALUE knob to select the file to be deleted.

Press the SET piston.

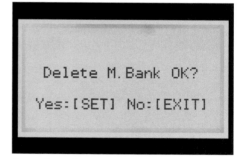

A confirmation message will appear. Press the SET piston again to delete the file. Push the EXIT knob if want to exit without deleting.

CHAPTER 8

Voicing & System Backups

Prerequisites

Ability to navigate the menus (see pp. vii and ix).

Chapter outline

- Basic concept
- When to make backups
- What's in a backup file?
- Managing your backup files
- File specifications
- Managing voicing files
- System back up and restore

8

Basic concept

Your Rodgers/Roland organ contains a variety of control settings that can be altered by you and/or your Rodgers/Roland representative. Collectively, these *configuration* settings are unique to your organ and determine many aspects of its performance and sound. It is essential to have a backup copy of this information (*data files*) in the event it needs to be reloaded. There are three types of backups that comprise the complete configuration of your organ:

- Combination memory
- Voicing data
- System data

When to make backups

The general rule of thumb is to make a backup whenever the configuration of your organ has changed. However, this could result in an excessive number of backups and become unwieldy to manage. There are, however, certain instances when a backup is essential:

- When your organ is initially installed, many system and voicing parameters are customized—be sure to make both a system and voicing backup.
- Make a new voicing backup whenever significant voicing changes are made. Keep any prior voicing backups in case you decide you want to revert to a prior voicing scheme. Document the date (and time if necessary) of voicing backups so that the precedence of each backup is clearly discernible.
- Back up combination memory levels when you have added new combination sequences for repertoire that you will perform again in the future.
- A complete system backup is imperative prior to any system software update being loaded. System and voicing parameters must be restored following a software update—you will want the system and voicing restored to the state it was in immediately prior to the software update. The back up and restore are part of the system software update process.

What's in a backup file?

In addition to combination memory backups (covered in *Chapter 7*), the other two types of data that comprise a complete copy of your organ's configuration are the voicing and system files.

Voicing

Your Rodgers/Roland organ is extensively voiceable. These voicing adjustments are what give your organ its unique sound in the space where it is installed. A complete voicing can take hours or even days to complete. Ultimately, the voicing configuration of your organ includes thousands of data elements. A backup of the voicing configuration is essential in the event that it needs to be reloaded. The voicing backup file includes:

- Current voicing settings
- Default Voice Palette
- MIDI coupler settings
- Library voice settings

In the event an organ is moved periodically and used in situations requiring unique voicing for each setup, an optimal voicing file can be created for each situation and simply loaded each time the organ is moved.

System data

In addition to combination memory and the voicing configuration, all other settings are part of the system parameters. These include:

- Audio settings
- Room Modeling settings
- Tutti settings
- Crescendo sequences
- Expression pedal settings
- MIDI settings
- Tremulant settings
- Console settings

8

Managing your backup files

Use separate memory sticks for each type of backup. For instance, use one memory stick for your combinations (see *Chapter 7*), a second memory stick for voicing backup, and a third memory stick for a system backup.

Get in the habit of carefully labelling each memory stick with detailed information about the organ model, type of backup and the date it was made. Although this approach to managing backups requires several memory sticks, the amount of data stored on any one stick is relatively small.

A memory stick with 256 megabyte (MB) capacity is generally more than enough memory for these purposes. These smaller memory sticks have the added advantage of being low cost—typically just a few dollars per memory stick. Although you may use larger memory sticks with several gigabytes (GB) of capacity, this is serious overkill for the task and incurs unnecessary expense.

File specifications

The various kinds of backups require different amounts of memory. Plus, a single USB stick will accommodate only a certain number of files for any given type of backup.

Use a separate memory stick for each type of backup. Refer to the following tables as you plan your backups.

Voicing

- One folder per memory stick

- Up to 999 voicing files may be saved—see **Appendix A** for instructions on naming files (the name you input is not shown in the file name on the memory stick—file names on the memory stick are generic)

- File size: 500KB - 1MB

File structure

📂 RODGERS

   🗎 VOICE001.DAT

   🗎 VOICE002.DAT

   🗎 VOICE003.DAT

   🗎 VOICE ...

   🗎 VOICE999.DAT

System

- One backup file per memory stick

- File size: 5MB +/-

File structure

📂 RODGERS

   📂 BACKUP

     🗎 BAKUP001.DAT

     🗎 ODSGN001.DAT

     🗎 PIPEI001.DAT

     🗎 SWASG001.DAT

     🗎 SYSTM001.DAT

     🗎 TUTTI001.DAT

     🗎 USER_001.DAT

     🗎 VOICE001.DAT

8

Voicing

- One folder per memory stick
- Up to 999 voicing files may be saved—see *Appendix A* for instructions on naming files (the name you input is not shown in the file name on the memory stick—file names on the memory stick are generic)
- File size: 500K - 1MB

File structure

🗁 RODGERS

   📄 VOICE001.DAT

   📄 VOICE002.DAT

   📄 VOICE003.DAT

   📄 VOICE ...

   📄 VOICE999.DAT

System

- One file per memory stick
- File size: 4MB +/-
- Note: system does *not* warn before overwriting a system back up file

File structure

🗁 RODGERS

   🗁 BACKUP

      📄 BAKUP001.DAT

Managing voicing files

All Rodgers organs use the same process for saving and loading voicing files. Up to 999 voicing files may be saved on a single memory stick, depending on the capacity of the memory stick.

Saving a voicing file to USB memory

Insert the memory stick before performing this procedure. Push the MENU knob and turn to navigate to *Save/Load USB* (Artist/Classic Menu 11, Infinity Menu 14). Push the SELECT knob to access the menu.

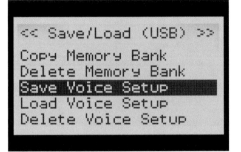

Turn the SELECT knob to highlight *Save Voice Setup*, and push to enter.

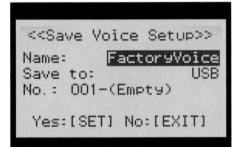

Turn the SELECT knob to highlight the *Name* parameter. Push the SELECT knob to access the screen where you can assign a custom name that identifies the voicing file being saved. See *Appendix A* for instructions on naming files.

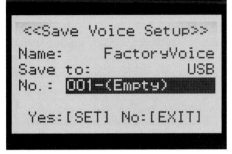

Turn the SELECT knob to highlight the *No.* parameter. Turn the VALUE knob to select a file number to save. If you don't want to overwrite an existing saved voicing file, choose a file number that indicates "Empty" (as shown above).

Press the SET piston to start the save. The window indicates the status of the save.

8

Loading a voicing file from USB memory

Before performing this procedure, insert a memory stick containing a voicing file you wish to load. *Note: the voicing file must be in the root [RODGERS] folder, not in a BACKUP folder.*

Push the MENU knob and turn to navigate to and highlight *Save/Load USB* (Artist/Classic Menu 11, Infinity Menu 14). Push the SELECT knob to access the menu.

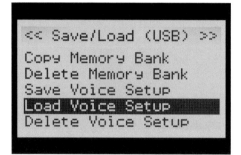

Turn the SELECT knob to highlight *Load Voice Setup*, and push to enter.

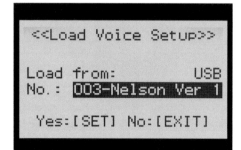

Turn the SELECT knob to highlight the *No.* parameter. Turn the VALUE knob to select the name of the voicing file you want to load.

Press the SET piston. A confirmation message appears. Press SET again to load.

Note: the voicing you just loaded is temporary. The organ will revert to its previous voicing when powered off and on again. If you wish to make the new voicing permanent, continue with the following instructions.

Press and hold SET, then press General Cancel (0). The Save Setup screen appears.

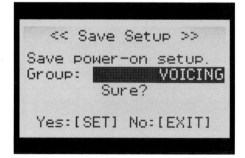

Turn the VALUE knob to select *VOICING* for the *Group* parameter. Press the SET piston. A confirmation message appears on the screen.

Deleting a voicing file from USB memory

Before performing this procedure, insert a memory stick into the organ containing a voicing file you wish to delete. *Note: the voicing file must be in the root [RODGERS] folder, not in a BACKUP folder.*

Push the MENU knob and turn to navigate to and highlight *Save/Load USB* (Artist/Classic Menu 11, Infinity Menu 14). Push the SELECT knob to access the menu.

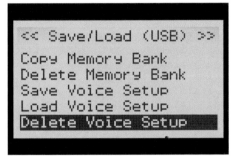

Turn the SELECT knob to highlight *Delete Voice Setup*, and push to enter.

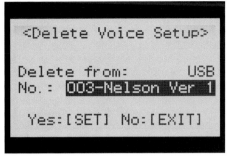

Turn the SELECT knob to highlight the *No.* parameter. Turn the VALUE knob to select the name of the voicing file you want to delete.

Press the SET piston. A confirmation message appears. Press SET again to delete.

System backup and restore

All Rodgers/Roland organs use the same process for backing up and restoring the system files. Only one system backup may be saved per memory stick. It is recommended that you use a blank memory stick. However, if you do not need to keep the previous system backup, you may use the memory stick previously used for backup. *The previous backup files on the memory stick will be overwritten.*

All Models

System backup to USB memory
Before performing this procedure, insert an empty memory stick. Push the MENU knob then turn to navigate to and highlight *Utility*. Push the SELECT knob to access the menu. Turn the SELECT knob to highlight *Backup/Restore*, and push to enter.

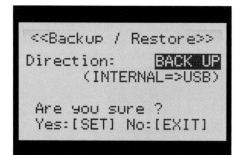

Turn the VALUE knob to select *BACK UP*.

Artist/Classic: Press the SET piston.

Infinity: Press the SET piston. A confirmation message appears. Press SET again to save the backup.

System restore from USB memory
Before performing this procedure, insert a memory stick containing a system backup file you wish to restore. Push the MENU knob then turn to navigate to and highlight *Utility*. Push the SELECT knob to access the menu. Turn the SELECT knob to highlight *Backup/Restore*, and push to enter.

Turn the VALUE knob to select *RESTORE*.

Press the SET piston. A confirmation message appears. Press SET again to load.

Appendix A Assigning File Names

When saving files internally or to external memory, you have the option to name the file for easy identification later. Follow the instructions below to name a file.

All Models

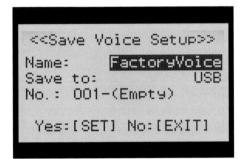

With the Name parameter highlighted, push the SELECT knob. The Rename window is displayed (below).

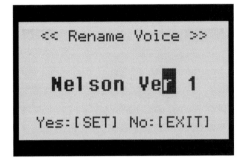

When you have finished entering the new name, press SET to save the name.

Push the EXIT knob to exit without saving.

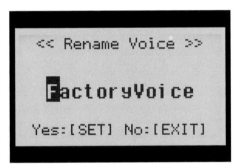

Turn the SELECT knob to move the cursor (the highlighted letter) to the left or right. Turn the VALUE knob to change the character at the cursor location. Refer to the character map on the next page.

The following characters are available for naming files:

A B C D E F G H I J K L M
N O P Q R S T U V W X Y Z

a b c d e f g h i j k l m
n o p q r s t u v w x y z

0 1 2 3 4 5 6 7 8 9

! & $ # @ *(space)* + -
% = . ' ( ) [ ] { } ^ _ `

When entering letters, use the M- piston to delete a character and the M+ piston to insert a space.

Appendix B Organ Type Specifications

The Organ Type feature described in *Chapter 2* is available on Infinity and 588 / 589 / 599 / 4589 models. This feature enables instantly changing the overall specification of the organ from the American Classic default to one of the following tonal styles:

- American Eclectic
- English Cathedral
- French Romantic
- German Baroque

These tonal stylings are achieved by using a particular Voice Palette voice for each stop. For your reference, a detailed listing of the Voice Palette selections for each organ type for Models 588 / 589 / 599 and Infinity 361 can be found on the following pages. The stops shown in blue indicate the alternate Voice Palette voice that is used.

Please note that the Organ Types are not "hardwired" specifications, i.e., the Voice Palette selection for any particular stop will be changed by other actions that change the Voice Palette selection subsequent to selecting an organ type. Refer to *Chapter 5* for more information on actions that change the voice state of a stop.

Because of the flexibility the Voice Palette provides, you can use the organ type as a starting point for creating your own custom specifications. Select the organ type you wish to start with, then change the Voice Palette selection on the stops for which you want to use a different voice, including any of the voices available on the Library/User stops. Save your edited organ type specification to a general piston for future use (see *Power Player Tip* on p. 15).

Infinity 361 Organ Type Specifications

American Eclectic	English Cathedral	French Romantic	German Baroque
Great			
Montre 16′ (VP0)	Montre 16′ (VP0)	Montre 16′ (VP0)	Prestant 16′ (VP2)
Principal 8′ (VP0)	Open Diapason 8′ (VP1)	Montre 8′ (VP3)	Octave 8′ (VP2)
Flûte Harmonique 8′ (VP0)	Gemshorn Celeste 8′ (VP1)	Flûte Harmonique 8′ (VP0)	Gemshorn Celeste 8′ (VP1)
Chimney Flute 8′ (VP0)	Chimney Flute 8′ (VP0)	Bourdon 8′ (VP1)	Rohrgedeckt 8′ (VP2)
Gemshorn 8′ (VP0)	2nd Diapason 8′ (VP1)	Gamba 8′ (VP3)	Salicional 8′ (VP2)
Octave 4′ (VP0)	Octave 4′ (VP0)	Principal 4′ (VP1)	Octav 4′ (VP2)
Open Flute 4′ (VP1)	Open Flute 4′ (VP1)	Spitzföte 4′ (VP0)	Rohrpfeife 4′ (VP2)
Quinte 2-2/3′ (VP0)	Quinte 2-2/3′ (VP0)	Tierce Mixture V (VP1)	Quinte 2-2/3′ (VP0)
Super Octave 2′ (VP0)	Super Octave 2′ (VP0)	Doublette 2′ (VP3)	Superoctav 2′ (VP2)
Fourniture V (VP0)	Fourniture XI (VP3)	Fourniture XI (VP3)	Mixtur IV (VP2)
Trumpet 8′ (VP1)	Trumpet 8′ (VP1)	Trompete 8′ (VP0)	Trompete 8′ (VP0)
Swell			
Bourdon Amabile 16′ (VP0)	Contre Gambe 16′ (VP1)	Bourdon Amabile 16′ (VP0)	Contre Gambe 16′ (VP1)
Diapason 8′ (VP0)	Geigen Diapason 8′ (VP1)	Diapason 8′ (VP0)	Geigen Diapason 8′ (VP1)
Bourdon 8′ (VP0)	Stopped Diapason 8′ (VP1)	Bourdon 8′ (VP0)	Bourdon 8′ (VP0)
Flute Céleste II 8′ (VP0)	Unda Maris II 8′ (VP1)	Flute Céleste II 8′ (VP0)	Unda Maris II 8′ (VP1)
Viole Céleste II 8′ (VP0)	Gamba Celeste II 8′ (VP1)	Viole Céleste II 8′ (VP0)	Schwebung II 8′ (VP3)
Prestant (VP0)	Viol Octave 4′ (VP1)	Prestant (VP0)	Prestant (VP0)
Flûte Traversière 4′ (VP0)	Flûte Traversière 4′ (VP0)	Flûte Traversière 4′ (VP0)	Flûte Traversière 4′ (VP0)
Nazard 2-2/3′ (VP0)	Twelfth 2-2/3′ (VP1)	Nazard 2-2/3′ (VP0)	Twelfth 2-2/3′ (VP1)
Octavin 2′ (VP0)	Fifteenth 2′ (VP1)	Octavin 2′ (VP0)	Fifteenth 2′ (VP1)
Tierce 1-3/5′ (VP0)	Cymbal VI (VP1)	Tierce 1-3/5′ (VP0)	Scherp III (VP2)
Chorus Mixture IV (VP0)	Plein Jeu IV (VP1)	Plein Jeu IV (VP1)	Grosse Fourniture III (VP3)
Double Trumpet 16′ (VP0)	Double Trumpet 16′ (VP0)	Bombarde 16′ (VP2)	Fagotto 16′ (VP3)
Trumpet 8′ (VP0)	Trumpet 8′ (VP0)	Trompette 8′ (VP2)	Trompette 8′ (VP1)
Hautboy 8′ (VP0)	Hautboy 8′ (VP0)	Hautbois 8′ (VP1)	Hautbois 8′ (VP1)
Clarion 4′ (VP0)	Clarion 4′ (VP0)	Clairon 4′ (VP2)	Clairon 4′ (VP1)

American Eclectic	English Cathedral	French Romantic	German Baroque

Choir

American Eclectic	English Cathedral	French Romantic	German Baroque
Erzähler 16' (VP0)	Bourdon 16' (VP1)	Bourdon 16' (VP1)	Bourdon 16' (VP1)
Principal 8' (VP1)	Viole 8' (VP2)	Montre 8' (VP0)	Montre 8' (VP0)
Concert Flute 8' (VP1)	Concert Flute 8' (VP1)	Gedeckt 8' (VP2)	Gedeckt 8' (VP2)
Unda Maris II 8' (VP1)	Erzähler Céleste II 8' (VP0)	Erzähler Céleste II 8' (VP0)	Erzähler Céleste II 8' (VP0)
Principal 4' (VP0)	Fugara 4' (VP1)	Principal 4' (VP0)	Principal 4' (VP0)
Flute d'Amour 4' (VP1)	Flute d'Amour 4' (VP1)	Flute d'Amour 4' (VP1)	Flute d'Amour 4' (VP1)
Cornet III (VP0)	Nazard 2-2/3' (VP2)	Cornet III (VP0)	Cornet III (VP0)
Klein Octave 2' (VP0)	Klein Octave 2' (VP0)	Waldflöte 2' (VP2)	Waldflöte 2' (VP2)
Larigot 1-1/3' (VP0)	Larigot 1-1/3' (VP0)	Larigot 1-1/3' (VP0)	Larigot 1-1/3' (VP0)
Raushwerke IV (VP0)	Mixture V (VP1)	Mixture V (VP1)	Mixture V (VP1)
Clarinet 8' (VP1)	Clarinet 8' (VP1)	Basson 8' (VP2)	Basson 8' (VP2)
Tuba Imperial 8' (VP0)	Tuba Imperial 8' (VP0)	Fanfare Trumpet 8' (VP1)	Fanfare Trumpet 8' (VP1)

Solo

American Eclectic	English Cathedral	French Romantic	German Baroque
Flauto Mirabilis 8' (VP0)	Grand Diapason 8' (VP1)	Flute Travers Harmonique 8' (VP2)	Grand Diapason 8' (VP1)
Orchestral Flute 4' (VP0)	Major Octave 4' (VP1)	Mounted Cornet 8' (VP2)	Major Octave 4' (VP1)
Corno di Bassetto 16' (VP0)	Bombarde 16' (VP1)	Bombarde 16' (VP1)	Dulzian 16' (VP2)
French Horn 8' (VP0)	Trompette Harmonique 8' (VP1)	Baryton 8' (VP2)	Trompette Harmonique 8' (VP1)
English Horn 8' (VP0)	Tierce Mixture XVII (VP1)	Basset Horn 8' (VP2)	Tierce Mixture XVII (VP1)
Trompette en Chamade 8' (VP0)	Tuba Major 8' (VP1)	Trompette en Chamade 8' (VP0)	Llamadas II 16+8 (VP2)

Pedal

American Eclectic	English Cathedral	French Romantic	German Baroque
Principal Bass 32' (VP0)	Contra Principal 32' (VP1)	Principal Bass 32' (VP0)	Contra Geigen 32' (VP2)
Contra Bourdon 32' (VP0)	Contra Bourdon 32' (VP0)	Contra Bourdon 32' (VP0)	Untersatz 32' (VP1)
Contra Bass 16' (VP0)	Principal 16' (VP1)	Principal 16' (VP1)	Principal 16' (VP1)
Subbass 16' (VP0)	Subbass 16' (VP0)	Subbass 16' (VP0)	Unterbass 16' (VP1)
Bourdon Amabile 16' (VP0)	Bourdon Amabile 16' (VP0)	Bourdon Amabile 16' (VP0)	Quintaton 16' (VP1)
Violone 16' (VP0)	Violone 16' (VP0)	Violone 16' (VP0)	Violone 16' (VP0)
Octave 8' (VP0)	Principal 8' (VP1)	Octave 8' (VP0)	Principal 8' (VP1)
Violoncello 8' (VP0)	Violoncello 8' (VP0)	Violoncello 8' (VP0)	Violoncello 8' (VP0)
Gedakt Bass 8' (VP0)	Flute Ouverte 8' (VP1)	Flute Ouverte 8' (VP1)	Gedakt Bass 8' (VP0)
Choral Bass 4' (VP0)	Fifteenth 4' (VP1)	Choral Bass 4' (VP0)	Fifteenth 4' (VP1)
Mixture IV (VP0)	Quinte Flute 10-2/3' (VP2)	Mixture IV (VP0)	Hintersatz IV (VP1)
Contre Bombarde 32' (VP0)	Ophicleide 32' (VP1)	Contre Bombarde 32' (VP0)	Bass Posaune 32' (VP2)
Bombarde 16' (VP0)	Double Trumpet 16' (VP1)	Bombarde 16' (VP0)	Posaune 16' (VP2)
Trompette 8' (VP0)	Trumpet 8' (VP1)	Trompette 8' (VP0)	Trompette 8' (VP0)
Clarion 4' (VP0)	Clarion 4' (VP1)	Clarion 4' (VP0)	Clarion 4' (VP0)

Model 588 / 589 / 599 Organ Type Specifications

American Eclectic	French Romantic	English Cathedral	German Baroque
Choir (Manual I)			
Spitz Principal 8' (VP0)	Montre 8' (VP1)	English Diapason 8' (VP2)	Spitz Principal 8' (VP0)
Still Gedackt 8' (VP0)	Bourdon 8' (VP1)	Bourdon 8' (VP1)	Rohr Gedackt 8' (VP3)
Unda Maris II 8' (VP0)	Unda Maris II 8' (VP0)	Unda Maris II 8' (VP0)	Unda Maris II 8' (VP0)
Spitzflöte 4' (VP0)	Flûte d'Amour 4' (VP2)	Spitzflöte 4' (VP0)	Spitzflöte 4' (VP0)
Principal 2' (VP0)	Doublette 2' (VP1)	Principal 2' (VP0)	Schwegel 2' (VP2)
Quinte 1 1/3' (VP0)	Nazard 2 2/3' (VP3)	Quinte 1 1/3' (VP0)	Quinte 1 1/3' (VP0)
Sesquialtera II (VP0)	Dolce Cornet II (VP1)	Dolce Cornet II (VP1)	Sesquialtera II (VP0)
Grave Mixture IV (VP2)	Mixtur III (VP0)	Grave Mixture IV (VP2)	Mixtur III (VP0)
Clarinette 8' (VP1)	Cromorne 8' (VP0)	Clarinette 8' (VP1)	Bärpfeife 8' (VP3)
Fanfare Trumpet 8' (VP0)	Trompet II 16'+8' (VP3)	Royal Tuba 8' (VP1)	Fanfare Trumpet 8' (VP0)
Great (Manual II)			
Violone 16' (VP0)	Bourdon 16' (VP2)	Principal 16' (VP1)	Quintaton 16' (VP3)
Principal 8' (VP0)	Montre 8' (VP2)	Open Diapason 8' (VP1)	Prinzipal 8' (VP3)
Gemshorn 8' (VP0)	Gemshorn 8' (VP0)	2nd Diapason 8' (VP1)	Voce Umana II 8' (VP2)
Gedackt 8' (VP0)	Gedackt 8' (VP0)	Clarabella 8' (VP1)	Gedackt 8' (VP0)
Principal 4' (VP1)	Octava 4' (VP0)	Principal 4' (VP1)	Octava 4' (VP0)
Quinte 2 2/3' (VP0)	Quinte 2 2/3' (VP0)	Twelfth 2 2/3' (VP1)	Quinte 2 2/3' (VP0)
Superoctav 2' (VP0)	Fifteenth 2' (VP1)	Fifteenth 2' (VP1)	Superoctav 2' (VP0)
Mixtur IV (VP0)	Mixtur IV (VP0)	Rauschquint IV (VP3)	Mixtur IV (VP0)
Trumpet 8' (VP0)	Trompette 8' (VP2)	Trumpet 8' (VP0)	Krumhorn 8' (VP3)

American Eclectic	French Romantic	English Cathedral	German Baroque

Swell (Manual III)

American Eclectic	French Romantic	English Cathedral	German Baroque
Geigen Diapason 8′ (VP0)	Geigen Diapason 8′ (VP0)	Geigen Diapason 8′ (VP0)	Geigen Diapason 8′ (VP0)
Flûte Harmonique 8′ (VP1)	Flûte Harmonique 8′ (VP1)	Flûte Harmonique 8′ (VP1)	Bourdon 8′ (VP0)
Viola Celeste II 8′ (VP0)	Viola Celeste II 8′ (VP0)	Viola Celeste II 8′ (VP0)	Viola Celeste II 8′ (VP0)
Principal 4′ (VP0)	Prestant 4′ (VP2)	Principal 4′ (VP0)	Principal 4′ (VP0)
Flûte traversière 4′ (VP0)	Flûte traversière 4′ (VP0)	Solo Flute 4′ (VP1)	Nachthorn 4′ (VP3)
Nasat 2 2/3′ (VP0)	Nazard 2 2/3′ (VP2)	Twelfth 2 2/3′ (VP1)	Nasat 2 2/3′ (VP0)
Piccolo 2′ (VP0)	Doublette 2′ (VP2)	Fifteenth 2′ (VP1)	Fifteenth 2′ (VP1)
Tierce 1 3/5′ (VP0)	Tierce 1 3/5′ (VP0)	Tierce 1 3/5′ (VP0)	Terz 1 3/5′ (VP2)
Plein Jeu IV (VP0)	Fourniture V (VP2)	Plein Jeu IV (VP0)	Scherp III (VP3)
Basson 16′ (VP0)	Bombarde 16′ (VP2)	Double Trumpet 16′ (VP1)	Dulzian 16′ (VP3)
Hautbois 8′ (VP0)	Trompette 8′ (VP2)	Hautbois 8′ (VP0)	Schalmei 8′ (VP3)

Pedal

American Eclectic	French Romantic	English Cathedral	German Baroque
Contre Bourdon 32′ (VP2)	Montre 32′ (VP0)	Montre 32′ (VP0)	Contra Geigen 32′ (VP1)
Principal 16′ (VP0)	Contrebasse 16′ (VP2)	Open Wood 16′ (VP1)	Principal 16′ (VP0)
Subbass 16′ (VP0)	Subbass 16′ (VP0)	Subbass 16′ (VP0)	Subbass 16′ (VP0)
Octave 8′ (VP1)	Montre 8′ (VP2)	Octave 8′ (VP1)	Octava 8′ (VP0)
Bourdon 8′ (VP0)	Bourdon 8′ (VP0)	Stopped Flute 8′ (VP1)	Still Gedackt 8′ (VP3)
Choral Bass 4′ (VP0)	Choral Bass 4′ (VP0)	Fifteenth 4′ (VP1)	Fifteenth 4′ (VP1)
Trombone 16′ (VP1)	Bombarde 16′ (VP2)	Trombone 16′ (VP1)	Posaune 16′ (VP0)
Trumpet 8′ (VP1)	Trompette 8′ (VP2)	Trumpet 8′ (VP1)	Trompete 8′ (VP0)
Klarine 4′ (VP0)	Cornet Clarion 4′ (VP1)	Klarine 4′ (VP0)	Klarine 4′ (VP0)

Appendix C Library / User Voice Lists

Voice numbers apply to Rodgers/Roland models as follows:

- *I* = Infinity: 243x / 361x / 484x
- *A* = Artist: 579 / 589 / 599 / 4589
- *C/5x8* = Classic: C-330 / C-380 / 558 / 568 and 578 / 588

Voice	I	A	C/5x8	Notes
Principal 32	001	001	1	
Contra Geigen 32	002	002	2	
Contra Bourdon 32	003	003	3	
Prestant 16	004			
Spitz Prinzipal 16	005	004	4	
Lieblich Gedackt 16	006	005	5	
Dulciana 16	007	006	6	
2nd Dulciana 16	008			
Cellos Céleste II 16	009	007	7	
Erzhaler Céleste II 16	010	008	8	
Stentorphone 8	011			
Principal 8	012			
Octave 8	013			
Montre 8	014	009	9	
Bach Principal 8	015	010	10	
Gemshorn-1 8	016	011	11	
Gemshorn-2 8	017			
Gamba 8	018	012	12	
Céleste III 8	019	017	17	
Violes des Anges II 8	020			
Salicional 8	021			
Unda Maris III 8	022	018	18	
Dulciana 8	023	013	13	
Aeoline 8	024			
Aeoline Céleste II 8	025			

Voice	I	A	C/5x8	Notes
Holzgedackt 8	026	014	14	
Gross Flute 8	027	015	15	
2nd Flute Harmonique 8	028	016	16	
Quintadena 8	029			
Rohrgedackt 8	030			
Metal Gedackt 8	031			
Octave 4	032			
Oktav 4	033			
Principal 4	034	019	19	
Rohrflöte 4	035			
Orchestral Flute 4	036			
Open Flute 4	037	020	20	
Chimney Flute 4	038	021	21	
Quinte 2-2/3	039	022	22	
Nazard 2-2/3	040	023	23	
Gemshorn 2	041	024	24	
Piccolo 2	042	025	25	
Tierce 1-3/5	043	026	26	
Larigot 1-1/3	044	027	27	
Septième 1-1/7	045	028	28	
Sifflöte 1	046	029	29	
Jeu de Clochette II	047	030	30	
Gabler Cornet V	048	033	33	
Cornet des Violes III	049			
Pedal Grand Mixtur VI	050	034	34	
Grave Mixtur IV	051	035	35	
2nd Grave Mixtur IV	052	036	36	
Grand Fourniture V	053			
Fourniture (San Sulpice) IV-VI	054	037	37	
Tierce Fourniture VI	055	038	38	
Grand Mixtur VIII	056	039	39	
Klein Mixture III	057			

Voice	I	A	C/5x8	Notes
Quartane II	058	031	31	
Scharf II	059	032	32	
Double Ophicleide 32	060	040	40	
Contre Bombarde 32	061	041	41	
Contre Bassoon 32	062	042	42	
2nd Bombarde 16	063	043	43	
Double Trumpet 16	064			
Contre Trompette 16	065	044	44	
Rankett 16	066	045	45	
Trompet 8	067	046	46	
Trompette 8	068	047	47	
2nd Trompette 8	069	048	48	
2nd Trumpet 8	070			
Trompette Harmonique 8	071			
French Horn 8	072			
Hautbois 8 (CC)	073			
Rohr Schalmei 8	074			
Douçaine 8	075			
Dulzian 8	076	051	51	
Cromorne 8	077	052	52	
Baryton 8	078	053	53	
Cor d'Amour 8	079	054	54	
Regal 8	080	055	55	
Vox Humana 8	081	056	56	
Vox Humaine 8	082	057	57	
Vox Humaine Trem 8	083	058	58	
Tuba Mirabilis 8	084			
State Trumpet 8	085	049	49	
Chamades 8	086	050	50	
Llamadas II 16+8	087			
Clarion 4	088	059	59	
Clairon 4	089	060	60	

Voice	I	A	C/5x8	Notes
2nd Clairon 4	090	061	61	
Rohrschalmei 4	091	062	62	
Principals III 8+4+2	092	063	63	
Principals+Mix 8+4+2+IV	093	064	64	
Full Swell 16+8+4+Reeds	094	071	71	
Flute Célestes IV 16+4	095	065	65	
Célestes IV 16+4	096	066	66	
Célestes VI 16+8+4	097	067	67	
Célestes VII 16+8+4+Vox	098	068	68	
Voxes II 16+8	099	069	69	
Voxes II 16+4	100	070	70	
Tibia 8	101	072	72	
Tibia 4	102	073	73	
VDO Celeste 8	103	074	74	
VDO Celeste Trem 8	104	075	75	
Tuba Trem 8	105	076	76	
Cornopean Trem 8	106	077	77	
Tibias 16+8+Vox 16+ 8	107	078	78	
Full Tibias+Strs 8+4	108	079	79	
Vox&Str 16+Tib 8+Quint	109	080	80	
Vox 16+8+Celetes 8	110	081	81	
Tibias 8,4+Str	111	082	82	
Tibias 8,4+Str	112	083	83	
Tibias 8,4+Tuba 8	113	084	84	
Tibia 4+Celestes 8	114	085	85	
Tibias 4,2+Str 16, 8	115	086	86	
Tibia 4 + Kinura 8	116	087	87	
Str 8+Tibias 2+Glocken	117	088	88	
Tibia 4+Glockenspiel	118	089	89	
Organ Harp 8	119	090	90	
Chrysoglott 4	120	091	91	
Tracker/Barker Noise	121	092	93	

Voice	I	A	C/5x8	Notes
Grand Piano	200	200		
Grand Piano 2	201			
Elec Piano	202	201		
Fantasia	203			
Harpsichord 8 I	204	202	98	
Harpsichord 8 II	205	203	99	
Harpsichord 4	206	204	100	
Harpsichord Lute	207	205	101	
Harpsichord 8+8	208	206	102	
Harpsichord 8+4	209	207	103	
Celesta	210	208	104	
Xylophone	211			
Orchestral Harp	212	209		
Drawbar 1	213	210		
Drawbar 2	214	211		
Guitar	215	212		
Acoustic Bass	216	213		
String Ensemble	217	214		
Smooth Strings	218			
Slow Strings	219	215		
Pizzicato	220			
Contra Basses	221			
Octave Strings	222	216		
Slow Violin/Cello	223	217		
Chamber Strings	224			
Violin/Cello	225			
Saxophone	226	218		
Saxophone 2	227			
Orchestral Trumpet	228	219	97	
Mellow Horn	229			
Brass Ensemble	230	220		
Cup Mute	231			

Voice	I	A	C/5x8	Notes
Bright Brass	232			
French Horn Section	233	221		
French Horn Solo	234			
Euphonium	235			
Orchestral Flute	236	222	96	
Pan Pipes	237			
Fifes	238			
Orchestral English Horn	239			
Bassoon/English Horn	240			
Orchestral Oboe	241	223	94	
Orchestral Clarinet	242	224	95	
Bagpipes	243			
Choir Aahs	244	225		
Choir Oohs	245	226		
Soprano Ah	246			
Organ Chimes	247	227		
Tubular Bells	248	228	92	
Tower Chimes	249	229		
Handbells	250	230		
Sleigh Bells	251			
Timpani	252	231		
Timpani Roll	253			
Percussion Set	254			
Ride Cymbal	255			
Crash Cymbal	256			
Orchestral Snare	257			
Snare Roll	258			

About the author

Nelson Dodge and his wife Claris are the owners of Church Keyboard Center in Pasadena, California, and the Rodgers/Roland Organs representatives for Southern and Central California since 2011. Please visit the web site at www.churchkeyboard.com.

Being a Rodgers/Roland organ dealer is the latest chapter in a career that has followed a varied path. Nelson has previously served as exec-utive director for a symphony orchestra, marketing director for a technology company, owner/president of an advertising agency, a marketing consultant, and a part-time church organist. In 1995 he completed an MBA degree at the Pepperdine University Graziadio School of Business and Management.

Nelson first played a new three-manual Rodgers organ in 1982 as a substitute organist at a church in Van Nuys, CA, and has been a fan of Rodgers organs ever since. Now, thirty years later, with Rodgers organs possessing vastly expanded capabilities and leading technology, he was inspired to write this *Guide* to help organists unlock the full potential of the current generation of Rodgers/Roland organs.

Church Keyboard Center was awarded the 2013 Kakehashi Award, presented by Rodgers Instruments in recognition of innovation and overall excellence as a Rodgers dealer.

The next edition

This book will be updated as new models and features are developed by Rodgers Instruments and Roland. Please send any suggestions for inclusion in future editions to nelson@churchkeyboard.com.

Where to get more copies of this book

Additional copies of the *Power Player's Guide* may be purchased from PowerPlayersGuide.com, Amazon.com and other online stores.

Made in the USA
Charleston, SC
21 January 2015